POEMS
TO AWAKEN YOUR SOUL

FORTY FOUR POEMS CHANNELLED FROM SOURCE TO BRING YOU PEACE, JOY AND AWAKENING

RUDI DE PONTE
DIMITRIOS KALOGEROPOULOS

POEMS
TO AWAKEN YOUR SOUL

FORTY FOUR POEMS CHANNELLED FROM SOURCE TO BRING YOU PEACE, JOY AND AWAKENING

All rights reserved. No part of this publication may be reproduced, stored in a retrieval system or transmitted in any form or by any means, electronic, mechanical, photocopying or otherwise, without the prior permission of the copyright owner.

All rights reserved.

No part of this book may be reproduced or transmitted in any form or by any means, electronic or mechanical, including photocopying, recording, or by any information storage or retrieval system, without permission in writing from the Publisher.

Publisher: KalosDePonte Publishing

Any unauthorized use, sharing, reproduction, or distribution of these materials by any means, electronic, mechanical, or otherwise is strictly prohibited. No portion of these materials may be reproduced in any manner whatsoever, without the express written consent of the publisher.

WAIVER: The author of this book does not dispense medical advice or other professional advice or prescribe the use of any technique as a form of diagnosis or treatment for any physical, emotional, or medical condition. The intent of the author is only to offer information of an anecdotal and general nature that may be part of your quest for emotional and spiritual wellbeing. In the event you or others use any of the information or other content in this book, the author and the publisher assume no responsibility for the direct or indirect consequences. The reader should consult his or her medical, health, or other professional before adopting any of the suggestions in this book or drawing inferences from it.

PREFACE

In the quiet corners of our hearts and the depths of our thoughts, there exists an innate longing to connect with something greater, something profound and timeless. It is within these sacred spaces that poetry finds its purpose, as a vessel for the soul's yearnings, a mirror to our emotions, and a guide on our journey of self-discovery.

"Poems to Awaken the Soul" is a collection that dares to traverse the delicate landscapes of human experience, illuminating the corners of joy, sorrow, love, and introspection. This anthology is a testament to the power of words, woven together with care and intention, to elicit emotions, provoke thought, and ultimately, to stir the dormant depths of our souls.

The poems within these pages are more than just verses; they are windows into the human condition. They encapsulate moments of vulnerability, resilience, and transcendence – a symphony of emotions that resonate across time, culture, and circumstance. Whether you find solace in the gentle embrace of nature's beauty, seek solace amid life's uncertainties, or yearn for connection in a world often disconnected, these poems offer a hand to hold and a voice to echo your own thoughts.

Each poem is a brushstroke, meticulously chosen to paint the canvas of the soul. They invite you to linger in their rhythm, ponder their meanings, and embark on a shared journey of awakening. As you delve into these verses, may you find familiarity in their cadence, and may they whisper to you the truths that lie within, waiting to be discovered.

"Poems to Awaken the Soul" is an offering, a collection of heartfelt expressions that seek to bridge the gap between the mundane and the mystical. It is an invitation to reflect, to feel, and to embrace the richness of the human experience. So, dear reader, let these words weave their magic, let them stir your spirit, and let them awaken your soul to the beauty that resides both within and around you.

INTRODUCTION

In the hustle and bustle of our modern lives, we often find ourselves disconnected from the rhythm of our own souls and the profound energy that surrounds us. It is within the stillness that we can truly hear the whispers of our inner selves, and it is through intentional moments of reflection that we can awaken the dormant magic that resides within us all. Welcome to "Poems to Awaken the Soul."

In this collection, you will find more than mere verses on pages; you will discover an opportunity to embark on a transformative journey of self-discovery and connection. These poems are not meant to be hastily read and forgotten, but rather, they invite you to engage in a ritual of mindfulness. As the authors, Rudi de Ponte and Dimitri Kalogeropoulos, we encourage you to immerse yourself in the experience, to create a space of tranquility where the symphony of your breaths and the resonance of these words can intertwine.

Guided by our own exploration of various spiritual healing techniques and an innate connection to the universe, we have crafted these poems with a purpose beyond ink and paper. Each poem is accompanied by symbols placed intentionally on the left side – symbols that carry deep meaning, inviting you to meditate upon them as you read. As you allow your gaze to rest upon these symbols, let them become a portal to your own internal sanctuary, a focal point for your thoughts and emotions to converge.

To truly unlock the magic within these pages, we invite you to read each poem not just once, but three times. With each reading, take deep breaths, inhaling the essence of the words and exhaling the clutter of the mind. As you do so, let the symbols guide you deeper into the heart of the poem, connecting you with the essence of its message and the universe's energy that flows through you.

The poems in this collection touch upon the tapestry of human experience – from the mundane to the mystical, from the joyous to the contemplative. They are an invitation to delve into the layers of your own being, to explore the labyrinth of emotions that make you who you are. Through this exploration, you may find healing, clarity, and a sense of unity with the cosmos that surrounds you.

As you journey through these pages, remember that you are not alone. The universe is intricately woven into the fabric of your existence, and these poems are a testament to that connection.

So, find a quiet space, let the stillness envelop you, and embark on this voyage of awakening. May "Poems to Awaken the Soul" serve as a guide, a companion, and a catalyst for your own magical transformation.

Yours truly,

Rudi de Ponte

Dimitrios Kalogeropoulos

INDEX

SACRED CORD	1
PLAYFUL TIME	2
YES & NO	3
NUMBER 5	4
FROM MY HEART TO YOURS	5
RETURN TO CHILD	6
THE BOX WITH TREE LINES	7
THE TIME IS NOW	8
MORE THAN PYRAMIDS	9
EVERY DROP OF WATER	10
THE POWER OF SUN	11
THE GOLDEN OAK	12
FOUR ELEMENTS	13
CRYSTALS	14
SOUNDS	15
YOUR MANTRA	16
START THROUGH DETOX	17
MY MIRROR	18
BREATH	19
BLOWING ROSES	20
BURN SAGE BURN	21
ORIONS BELT	22

INDEX

MOON	23
DIVINE LIGHT	24
NOT JUST WORDS	25
NUMBERS EVERYWHERE	26
REIKI ENERGY	27
FIVE POINTED STAR	28
SAINT GERMAIN	29
THE ANGELIC REALM	30
SAINT PANTELEIMON	31
JESUS - SANADA	32
ISHTAR	33
GODDESS OF LIFE	34
LORD SHIVA	35
GANESH	36
SHAMANS WAY	37
ANIMAL SPIRITS	38
DRAGONS	39
MANIFESTING WITH 28	40
EMERALD TABLET	41
METATRON'S CUBE	42
PLEIAIDEANS	43
HEALING IN LABRYNTHS	44

These poems were written for you

1
SACRED CHORD

Beneath the tapestry of cosmic night,
where stars alight with shimmering light.
My birth's sweet moment, a sacred chord,
connects me to the universe's grand accord.

Born under constellations' watchful eyes,
planetary dances in celestial skies.
A map of destiny, a script unfurled,
guiding me through life's intricate swirl.

A date in time, a nexus of fate,
reveals the path I'm meant to skate.
As planets align in rhythmic chime,
whispering secrets of the cosmic prime.

From rising sun to moon's gentle glow,
each aspect's wisdom begins to show.
My strengths, my challenges, the journey ahead,
a tapestry woven in stars' silvery thread.

Mercury's wit, communication's grace,
Venus's love, an embracing embrace.
Mars's fire, igniting the will,
Jupiter's expansiveness, dreams to fulfill.

Saturn's lessons, a structured frame,
Uranus sparks change, an electric flame.
Neptune's mysteries, intuition's guide,
Pluto's transformations, where old worlds collide.

Through birth's true point, I find the key,
to unlock the door of authenticity.
With clarity's lantern, I navigate,
life's boundless sea, I no longer hesitate.

In starlit guidance, I shall confide,
trusting the Cosmos as my steadfast guide.
Birth's point of origin, a compass true,
I step into the world, my purpose in view.

2
PLAYFUL TIME

Playful time, oh, how sweet you are when you remain still,
In those tranquil moments, my soul finds a thrill.

Playful time, when you start to race and run,
You slip through my grasp, like the setting sun.

Yet, I beseech you, time, to find a gentle stride,
To balance your pace, in your ceaseless ride.

Grant me your patience and the warmth of your embrace,
And I shall, in return, venerate your grace.

Let us, time, be partners, in harmony and grace,
Share our energy, in this timeless space.

As you weave through life's intricate dance,
Leave a reminder for me, a tranquil trance.

Believe in me, and trust that I'll stand by your side,
In this world, where together, we'll eternally glide.

Smile at me, and I'll reflect your cheer,
Confidence and security will always be near.

My heart yearns for your equilibrium and peace,
May our connection and unity never cease.

Henceforth, I implore, do not borrow nor take,
But share as equals, for each moment we make.

Time, oh playful time, our bond shall be strong,
In this endless journey, where we both belong.

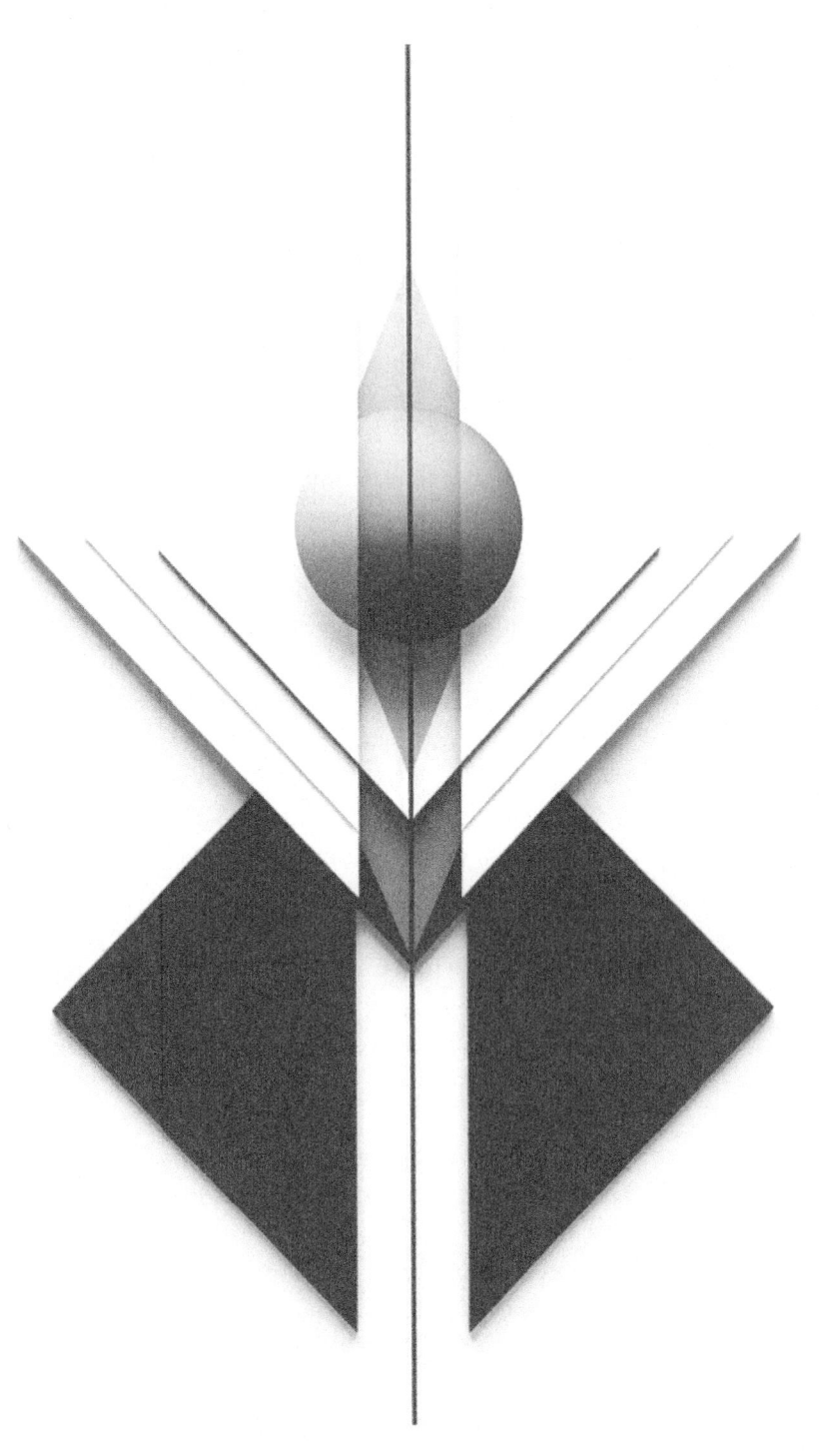

3
YES & NO

Imagine, I, the King of white light, wholeheartedly said yes,
Imagine, I, the King of darkness, firmly proclaimed no,
You and I, dear cosmos, are akin, this we must confess,
Yet humanity's view, starkly contrasts, doesn't it, though?

We share a purpose, both resolute and pure,
Yet the fruits we bear, often obscured, unsure.
"Love me as your light," said the King of pure white,
"Loathe me as your darkness," the inky void's plight.

We're but perceptions, responses, questions, and doubt,
Both positive and negative, alternating about,
The answers you seek, the choices you make,
Emit vibrations high and low, like waves on a lake.

Alter your gaze, treat us both with esteem,
We're the dual forces, recurring as a dream,
We're the resounding yes, the unyielding no,
We're what you desire, in the ebb and flow.

Peer past the mind, the ego's blindfold,
See us for what we are, a force untold,
Your reactions to us, pivotal in your tale,
Release the shackles of yes, and let no set sail.

In freedom, we thrive, as was destined to be,
Here to guide your earthly odyssey,
Tame your thoughts, find balance and poise,
We'll be your beacons, your infinite choice.

Together we'll journey, through time's endless stream,
In this cosmic dance, as light and dark gleam,
Imagine I, the King of white light, said yes,
Imagine I, the King of darkness, said no, nonetheless.

Seek the balance, align heart, soul, and mind,
In this dance with destiny, our essence intertwined,
Embrace both the light and the shroud of night,
For it's in the balance that you'll find your truest light.

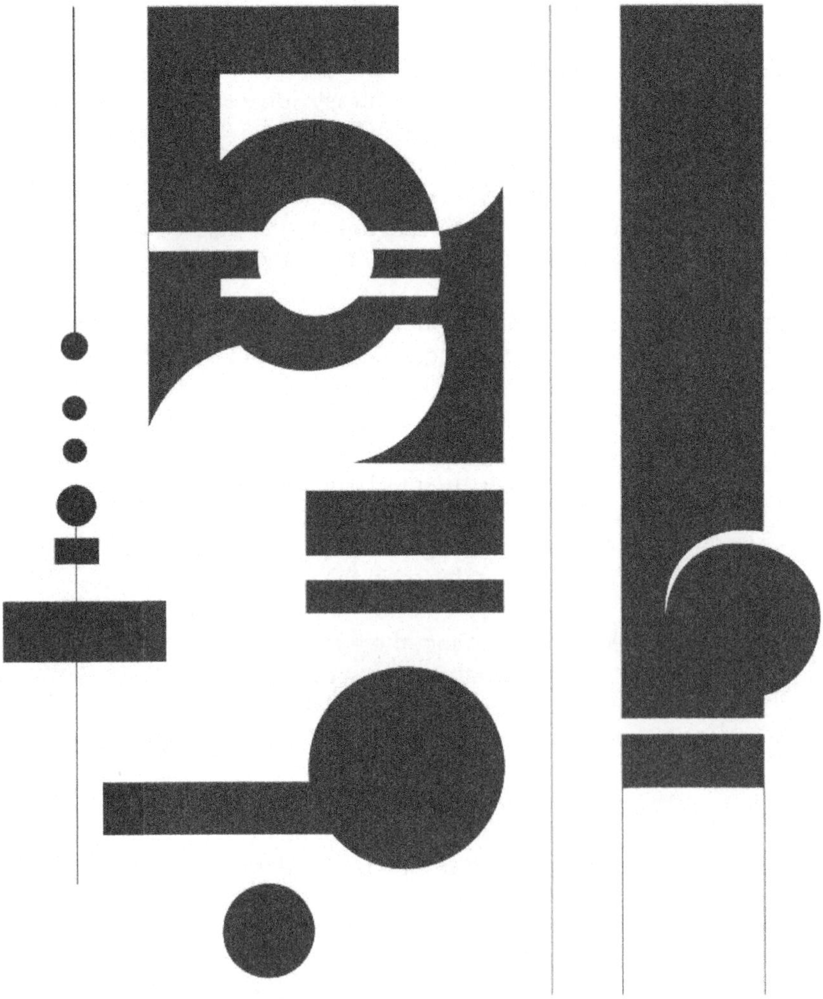

4
NUMBER 5

I move with a profound sense of purpose and action,
I am the embodiment of fire, the ardor from the south,
My spirit, a radiant crown, exudes satisfaction,
In harmony with soil, I blend with nature's gentle mouth.

Ego's ashes I temper with the water's gentle embrace,
Release me, exhale from the depths of your gut,
Witness me, as I ascend, leave without a trace,
Dissolving into the ether, like a fleeting sunset.

If you choose to sit in stillness with me,
I shall become your guide to destiny's decree,
Within the boundless cosmos, your place you'll see,
Fixed in time and space, your purpose shall be free.

I create from the heavens, alchemize your reality,
A co-creator of dreams, when you're still and free,
Watch as we weave wonders and manifest jointly,
Our souls intertwined in the grand tapestry.

Recall your birth, etched in your life's grand plan,
A design unburdened, attachments, you can ban,
Let experiences flourish, life's intricate strand,
In your unbounded journey, let your heart expand.

Oh, traveler of experiences, you I deeply cherish,
I love you unconditionally, and your journey, I nourish,
Honoring every moment, in which you may flourish,
Embracing the complexities, in life's symphony, we cherish.

I am Number 5, a cosmic entity, aligned with grace,
Guiding your voyage through time and infinite space,
With love, purpose, and profound embrace,
Our co-creation, an eternal, intricate embrace.

5
FROM MY HEART TO YOURS

Love, the Master of our existence, the radiant energy we obey,
This is the path we walk, come what may,
Love, the one true way, our guiding ray,
In its luminous presence, we shall forever stay.

When life confronts you with fear, anger, or sorrow's thief,
Whisper my name, let your heart find relief,
Call upon me, let your soul's compass be your belief,
From the depths of my heart, I'll mend your heart's grief.

Turn to me, from your heart to mine, make the plea,
I'll connect you to the source, in serenity,
A vibration so high, it sets your spirit free,
I transmute darkness into light, unequivocally.

In the face of turmoil, I stand undefeated, you'll see,
For there's no match for love, no greater decree,
Awaken within, unlock the truth, and be,
Boundless, limitless, for all eternity.

So call upon me, from your heart to mine, cease to sigh,
I am the infinite heart in the sky, the divine energy so high,
Filling you with hope, love, and joy, oh so nigh,
Lean on me, and your belief will touch the sky.

From my heart to yours, the love flows pure and bright,
Filling you with radiant beams of love and light,
Trust in me, dear traveler, take your flight,
In my embrace, you'll find endless delight.

Let my love be your compass, your guiding star,
In the vast cosmos, we are never too far,
Whisper my name, and you'll journey far,
In love's warm embrace, you'll find who you are.

Love, the eternal Master, the energy we adore,
In its profound embrace, we'll cherish evermore,
Love, our unwavering guide, our sacred lore,
In its arms, we'll forever soar.

6
RETURN TO CHILD

In the realm of innocence, so pure and bright,
where grown-up burdens take their flight,
A childlike heart, a boundless soul,
connects to cosmos, makes us whole.

With eyes aglow, like stars above,
we dance through fields, we laugh, we love,
No ego's weight to hold us down,
in laughter's embrace, we're free to drown.

Giggles rise like stardust's gleam,
a universe within, a wondrous dream,
Imagination paints the skies,
as carefree spirits start to rise.

Beneath the sun, on grassy ground,
a playground vast, where joy is found,
Swinging high as gravity sighs,
we touch the heavens with gleeful cries.

No clocks to watch, no time to fret,
just laughter's cadence, a sweet duet,
A bridge we build to galaxies far,
as childlike wonders guide our star.

Release the masks, the worries of years,
embrace the magic, conquer the fears,
For in the heart's playground, we reclaim,
the Universe's secret, a childlike aim.

So let us revel, let us play,
and shed the roles we wear each day,
In childlike rapture, we shall see,
the Universe dancing, wild and free.

7
THE BOX WITH THREE LINES

In the depths of your heart, seek me out,
Before your eyes, I stand with a box devout,
With three lines inscribed, I'm here to aid,
In protecting your wishes, helping you not to fade.

My energy, an eternal force, steadfast and true,
In my flesh and in my soul, love ever anew,
I stand unwavering, with compassion and care,
To mend your worries, and life's burdens bear.

Your sons and daughters, in their tender grace,
Bring them to me, in my loving embrace,
With the steadfast love and Christ's healing hand,
Together, we'll help them, we'll understand.

Take a sip from my box, with lines that shine,
Filled with light and love, transcending the confines of time,
Transmuting 'was' into 'is,' in faith's design,
Believe in me, as I believe in you, in life's grand rhyme.

Fear not, for by your side, I'll always reside,
A simple call, and I'll be your guide,
Seek me out, and there you shall confide,
With a smile, your fears shall subside.

I love you with the light of Christ, pure and bright,
For within you, the divine's radiant light,
Our connection, a bond, an unending flight,
In Christ's love, we'll find our way, forever in sight.

8
THE TIME IS NOW

In the realm of possibilities, the present lies,
no more excuses, let your spirit rise,
For the universe calls, its whispers clear,
it's time to step forward, cast away the fear.

The old you, a cocoon left behind,
emerges anew, in strength defined,
With courage ablaze, like a phoenix in flight,
igniting the darkness, embracing the light.

No more delays, no more holding back,
the Universe beckons, on the right track,
Shed the limitations, the doubts that constrain,
embrace your true path, let your essence reign.

The stars in the sky, the planets aligned,
hold the map to the life you've designed,
In harmony with cosmos, your purpose unfolds,
as you embrace the story your heart truly holds.

No more masks, no more pretense,
step into authenticity, with confidence,
The universe's symphony, your life's sweet song,
guiding you forward, helping you belong.

Connect with the energy that weaves the stars,
trust in the journey, no matter the scars,
Embrace the unknown, with arms open wide,
the Universe as your ally, walking by your side.

So let go of excuses, let go of the past,
embrace the adventure, feel the Universe's blast,
The time is now, to reveal the true you,
in the cosmic embrace, to your path, be true.

9
MORE THAN PYRAMIDS

In pyramids of ancient lore,
sacred knowledge they adore,
Whispers of the universe profound,
in stone and silence, secrets abound.

Beneath the starry cosmic dome,
builders etched wisdom in each stone,
Geometry and patterns divine,
revealing truths that intertwine.

Through corridors and chambers deep,
echoes of mysteries they keep,
Hieroglyphs in shadows dance,
inviting seekers to advance.

From galaxies to grains of sand,
inscribed in walls by master's hand,
The Universe's essence unfurled,
in pyramids, a cosmic world.

Gaze upon those ancient heights,
a gateway to celestial flights,
As seekers tread the hallowed floors,
they glimpse the Cosmos, its endless shores.

Let the pyramids stand as a guide,
to wisdom vast, never to hide,
In their silence, truths reside,
sacred knowledge, forever tied.

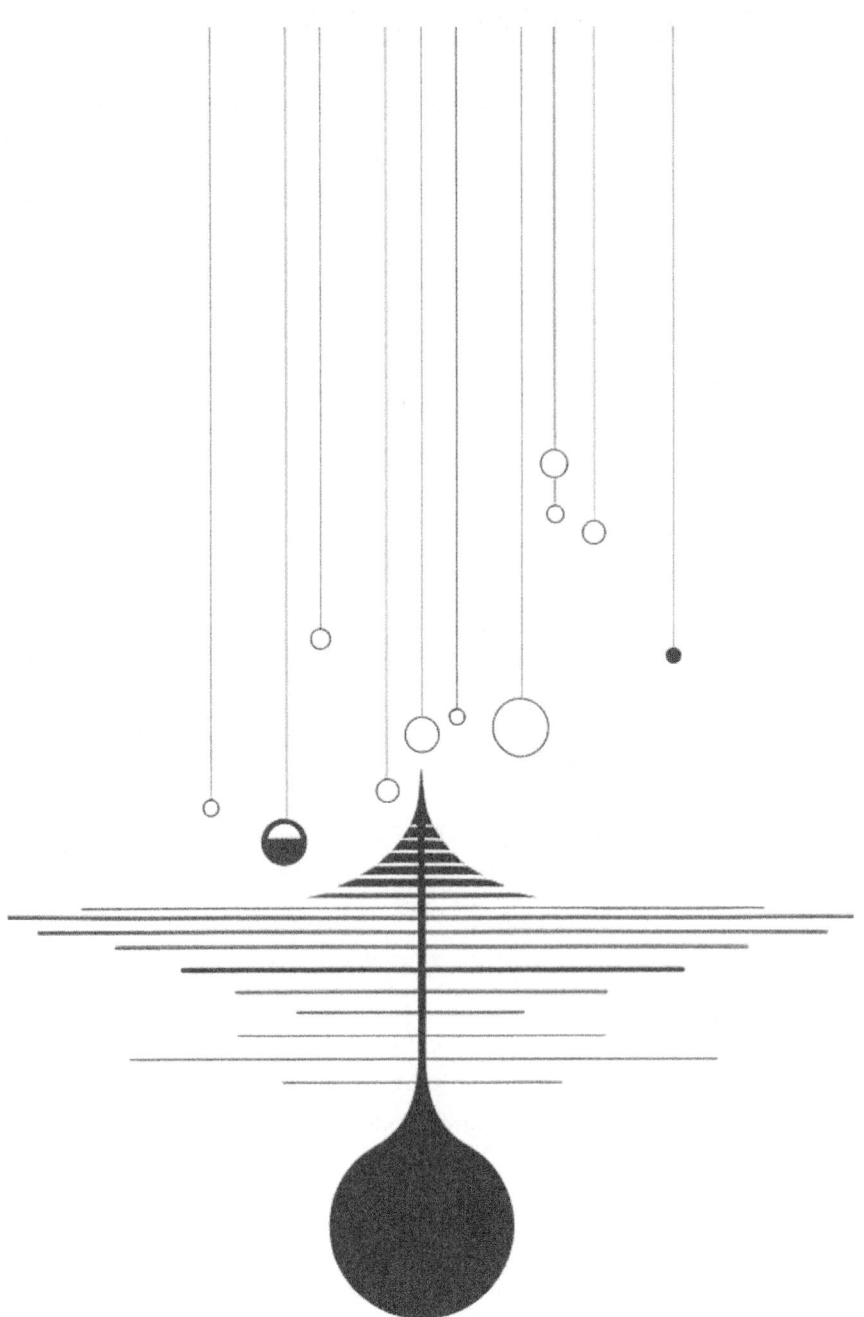

10
EVERY DROP OF WATER

Oh water, source of life and light,
in you, we find our strength and might.

Your healing powers, a wonder to behold,
a precious gift, more valuable than gold.

We give thanks to you, sea god and master,
for your unending grace and splendor,

You bring the rain, the rivers, and the sea,
you give us life, and set our spirits free.

Your waters flow, in a rhythm so divine,
a soothing balm, for the troubled mind,

Your waves embrace the shore with grace,
a tender stroke, our souls embrace.

Your essence, a symbol of gratitude and love,
a reminder, of blessings from above,

We honor you, in every drop and wave,
and thank you, for the life you save.

Oh water, we are forever in your debt,
for all the healing, and love you beget,

We give thanks to you, sea god and friend,
and pray that your blessings will never end.

11
THE POWER OF SUN

At dawn, when the sun rises high,
thirty degrees above the earth and sky.
I lift my face and close my eyes,
and thank the sun for its daily rise.

In the afternoon, when the day is bright,
and the sun is high, such a brilliant sight.
I pause and give thanks once more,
for the warmth and light that it pours.

As the sun begins to set in the west,
thirty degrees below, a peaceful rest.
I whisper my gratitude once again.
for holding me in my space, my friend.

I stand before you with my crown held high
ready for the light to enter me from above.
i recieve you and anchor your below. the
fire burns in the belly of the dragon.

Oh sun, you are a wonder to behold,
a source of life and energy, pure gold.
I thank the universe for your light,
and for holding me in my space so bright.

Three times a day, I bow my head,
and thank the sun for what is being fed.
My body, my soul, my very being,
thank you for holding me, sun, you are so freeing.

12
THE GOLDEN OAK

Amidst the rolling hills and verdant fields,
stands a golden oak tree, proud and wise.
Rooted deep in the earth, yet touching the skies,
its branches reaching out, its leaves unfurled.

This oak tree is more than just a tree,
it's a connection to the Universe and all that is.
A bridge between the earth and the heavens above,
a channel for the divine to speak to us.

For in its wisdom, the oak tree knows,
the secrets of the Cosmos, the ebb and flow.
The rhythms of life and the cycles of time,
and it whispers these truths to us in its own way.

Listen closely, and you'll hear its voice,
softly rustling in the breeze, a gentle noise.
But in its words, there is a power,
that can transform us at any given hour.

For when we connect with the wise gold oak tree,
we connect with the Universe and all that can be.
We tap into a source of infinite love,
and find within ourselves the wisdom from above.

So let us stand beneath its boughs,
and let its wisdom fill us now.
For in this oak tree, there is a key,
that can help unlock the mysteries of eternity.

13
FOUR ELEMENTS

Amid the elements, a dance unfolds,
a symphony of nature, ancient stories told.
In sea, in river, or tranquil lake's embrace,
I stand, a vessel, in this sacred space.

Beneath my feet, the earth's firm hold,
her heartbeat resonates, a story so bold.
With every step, I feel her pulse and sway,
grounding my spirit, in nature's grand display.

The water's touch, a gentle caress,
a liquid embrace, such a tranquil address.
It flows around, an essence so pure,
cleansing my soul, of that I'm sure.

The sun above, a warm embrace,
it's golden rays kiss my upturned face.
I bask in the light, its energy so grand,
a connection to Cosmos, as grains of sand.

The air around, a whispering breeze,
carries life's secrets through rustling trees,
Inhale its essence, let it fill my lungs,
a breath of life, from which all creation sprung.

Four elements merge, in harmonious blend,
around and within, where destinies mend.
But fifth is the spirit, transcendent and wise,
it enters my being, so that transformation may arise.

With an open heart, I invite it in,
this cosmic force that works from within.
Aligning my core, igniting the fire,
it elevates my spirit, taking me higher.

Earth, water, fire, and air unite,
with spirit's touch, their bonds ignite.
A symphony of elements, a soul's rebirth,
transforming me upon this sacred Earth.

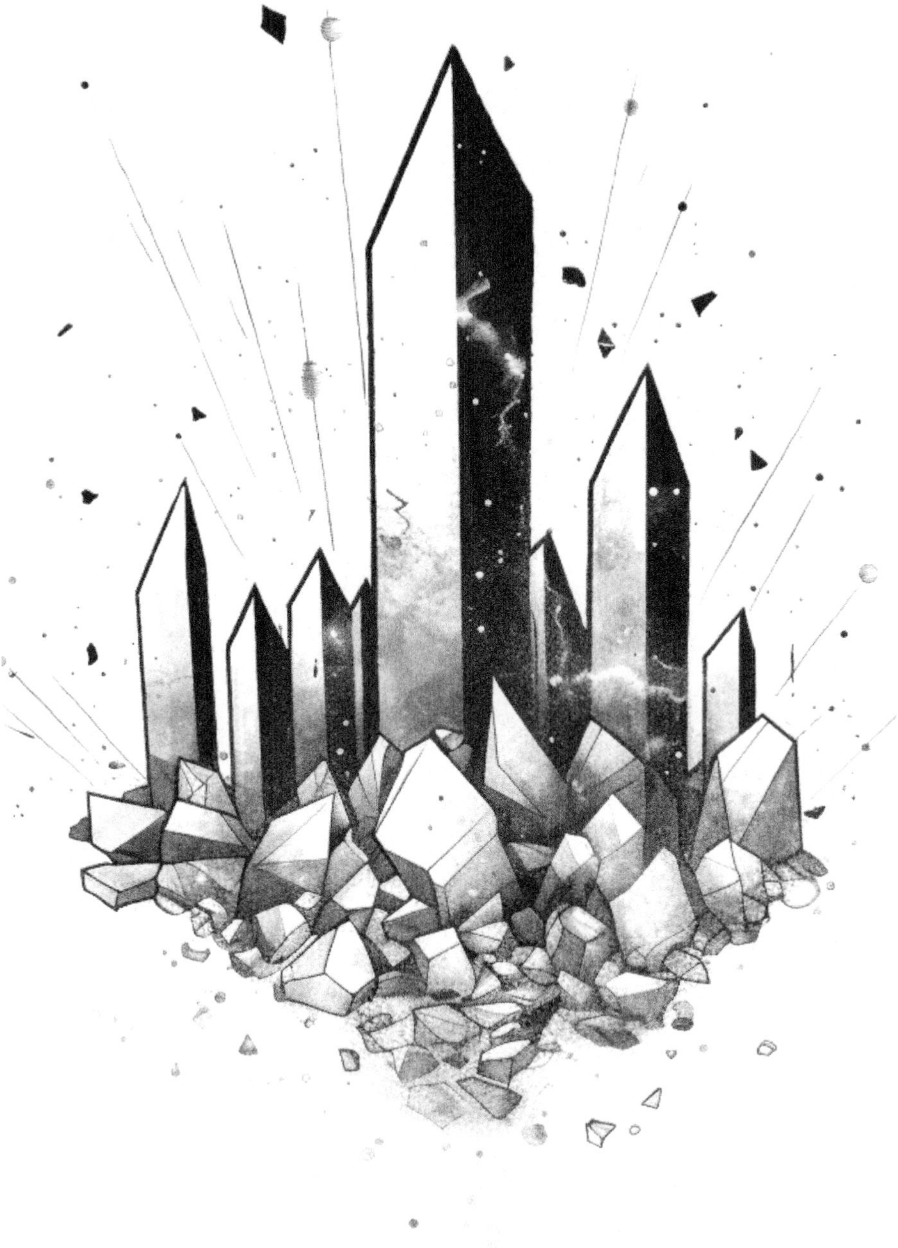

14
CRYSTALS

In crystals' depths, a world concealed,
energies waiting to be revealed.
With intention's touch, we write the script,
a healing dance, where energies are equipped.

Hold them close, in hands' embrace,
a sacred bond, a tranquil space.
With focused mind and heart aligned,
we program crystals, a love-defined bind.

Amidst the tapestry of Earth's ancient lore,
certain gems shine brighter than before.
Let's delve into the treasury, let's find the key,
to crystals' power, unshackled and free.

Amethyst's purple crown, a soothing guide,
calming the storms, where worries reside.
Clear Quartz, a canvas for intent's art,
amplifying energies from deep in the heart.

Rose Quartz, a tender embrace it brings,
healing all wounds, with love's soft wings.
Citrine's golden rays, like sunlit streams,
igniting abundance, fulfilling dreams.

Turquoise, a guardian of skies so vast,
a balm for the spirit, a refuge from the past.
Emerald's verdant grace, is nature's pure touch,
renewing the soul, with love's gentle clutch.

Onyx, a shield against negativity's hold,
a grounding force, where strength unfolds.
Moonstone's ethereal glow, emotions to sway,
guiding us through life's ever-changing ballet.

Labradorite's iridescence, a magical spark,
revealing unseen realms, when light's in the dark.
And Selenite's purity, like moonlit snow,
cleansing, uplifting, letting the energies flow.

So program these crystals, with love's pure embrace,
a symphony of healing, your own sacred space.
Unlock their potential, let the energies thrive,
as you journey within, and watch as your spirit comes alive.

Hz

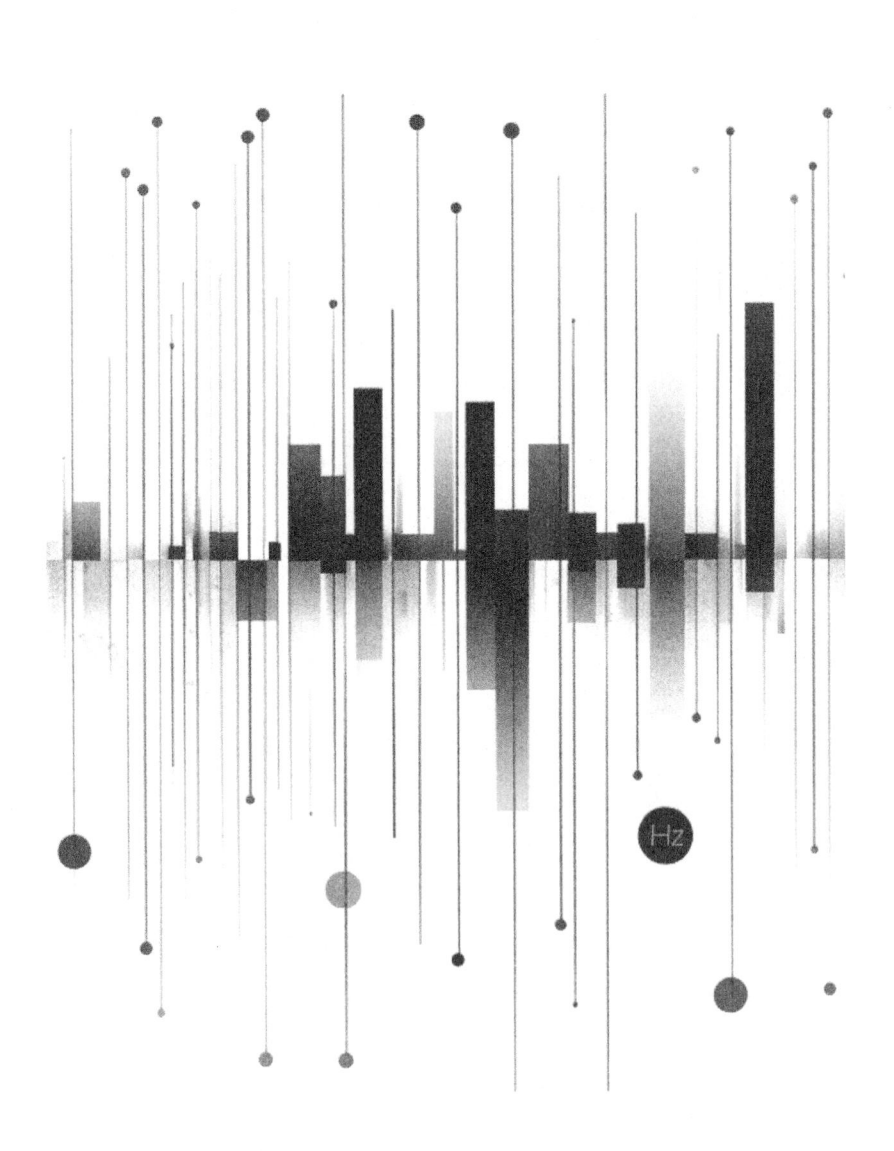

15
SOUND

In space where vibrations weave a sacred art,
a symphony of healing, a journey to the heart.
Sound waves ripple, like whispers through the air,
unlocking chakras' gates, a journey quite rare.

Begin with roots, where courage takes its stand,
the Muladhara, foundation of the grand.
Three-hundred sixty-six, the hertz it craves,
like red, its color grounds, and is where strength engraves.

Next, the Svadhisthana, the sacral's call,
orange hues, like sunsets' gentle fall.
Four hundred eighty-nine, its frequency aligns,
creative energies flow, as life designs.

Manipura's power, solar plexus aglow,
yellow brilliance, like sun's vibrant show.
Five hundred seventy-three, the magic tone,
empowerment awakens, as courage is sown.

The heart's Anahata, where love takes its flight,
green hues of compassion, all day and night.
Six hundred seventy-two, its frequency sings,
as healing waves embrace, on gentle wings.

Throat's Vishuddha, in shades of tranquil blue,
five hundred twenty-one, it resonates true.
Expressive energies flow, like the rivers' course,
authenticity is found, as voices endorse.

Anja, the third eye, where insights bloom,
indigo's mystery, a cosmic room.
Six hundred sixty-six, the pineal's grace,
intuition's embrace, as truth you face.

Lastly, the crown's Sahasrara, pure and white,
a portal to the cosmos, eternal light.
Seven hundred eighty-two, its frequency gleams,
connection to the divine, just like in dreams.

Sound frequencies as keys, each chakra to unseal,
colors weave their magic, their secrets to reveal.
As vibrations dance, and frequencies align,
chakras open, heal, and in their brilliance shine.

So let the symphony of sound waves play,
a healing journey, through night and day.
In harmonious flow, your chakras align,
a transformation profound, that is cosmic design.

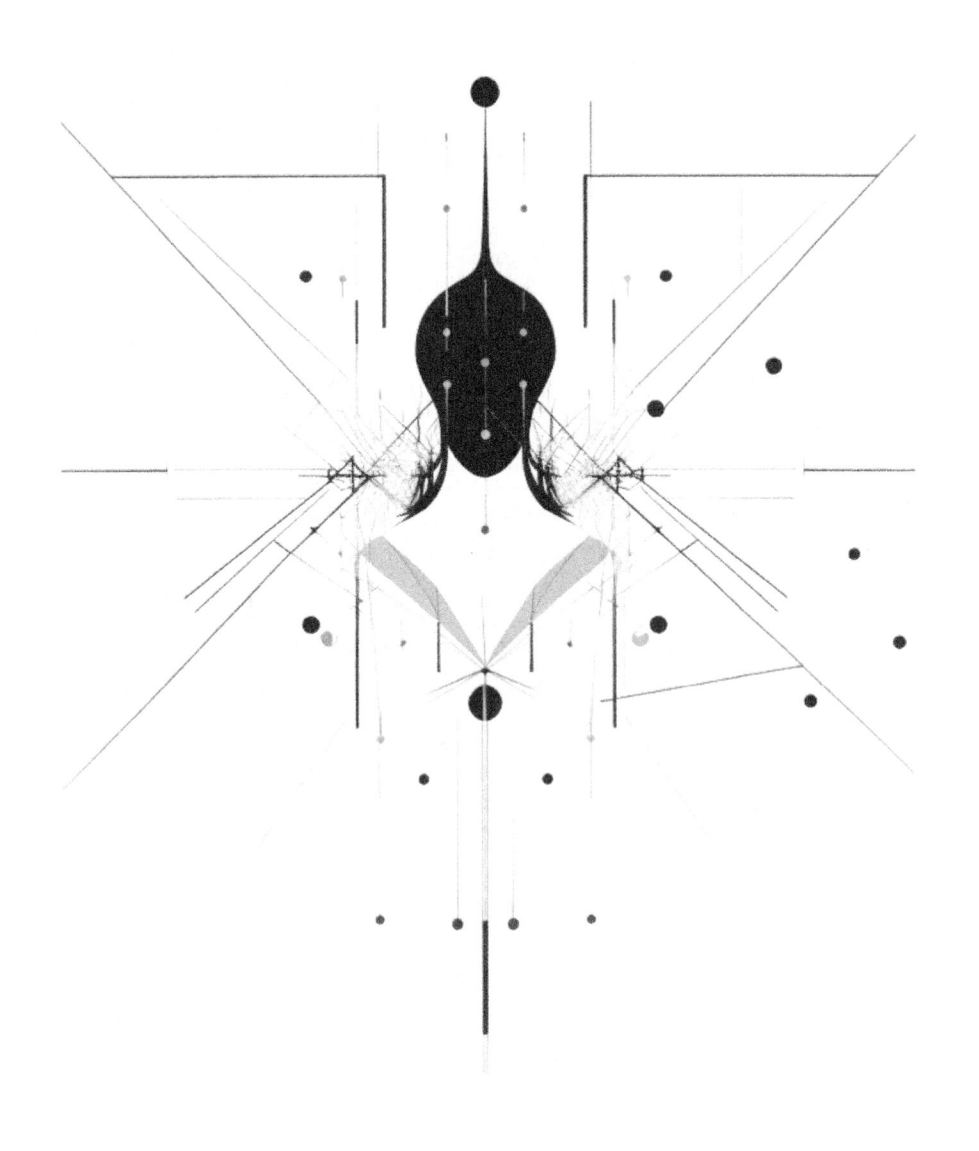

16
YOUR MANTRA

In the depths of silence, where whispers reside,
a mantra awaits, a treasure to guide.
A vibration of truth, a sacred sound,
in seeking its essence, connection is found.

With introspection's lantern, we explore,
to find our mantra, a portal to more.
Within our hearts' chamber, it gently awaits,
a key to the Universe, unlocking its gates.

Listen to the rhythm of your breath's gentle flow,
in the stillness, the answers will slowly show.
Seek the words that resonate deep within,
a mantra's birthplace, where intentions begin.

With every inhale, with every release,
let the mantra's melody offer you peace.
A bridge to the divine, to God's sacred space,
a communion of souls, an intimate embrace.

Repeat it like a prayer, with devotion sincere,
as God's energy flows, drawing you near.
In each whispered repetition, a cosmic dance,
you connect with the Source, in every glance.

Let your mantra be a guide, a compass true,
navigating existence, a constant renew.
A thread to the infinite, a song of the soul,
uniting with God, feeling eternally whole.

So find your mantra, a gift to embrace,
a spiritual journey, a celestial chase.
In its cadence, connection takes flight,
a union with God's energy, pure and bright.

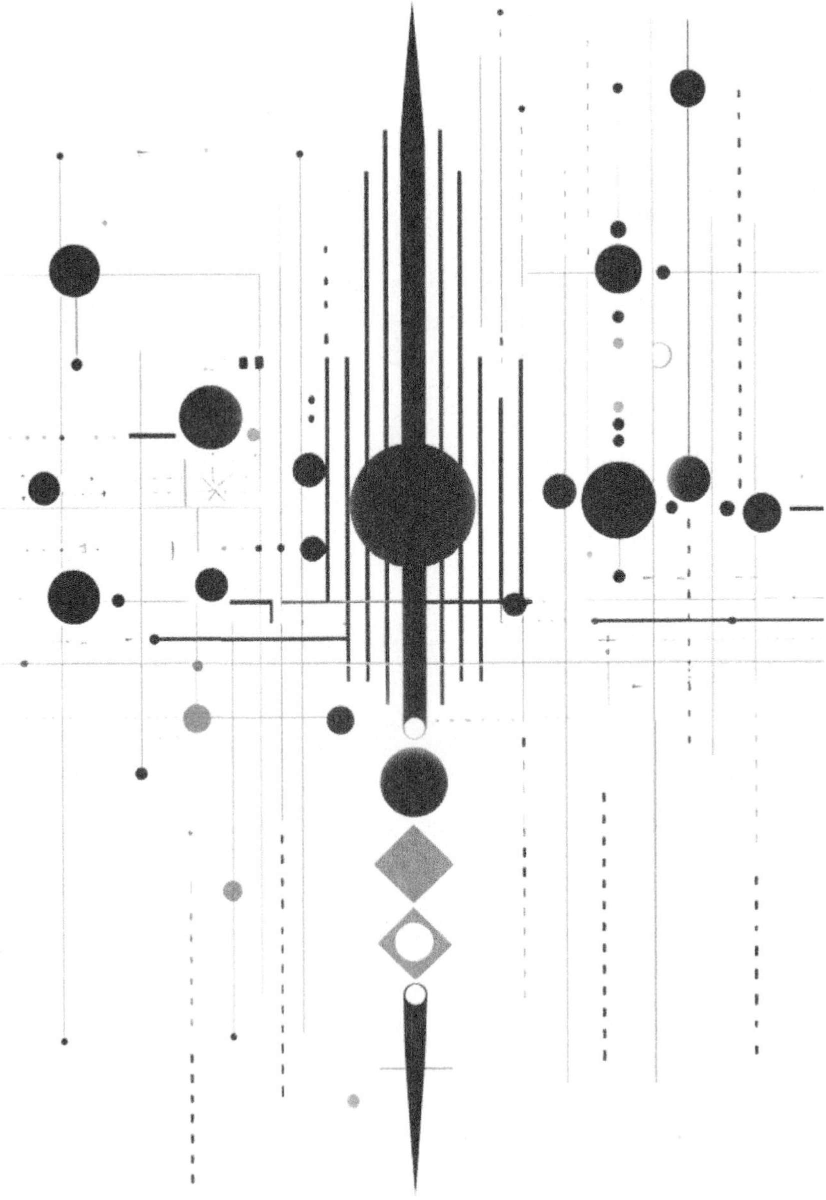

17
START THROUGH DETOX

In the realm of nourishment, a path unfolds,
a spiritual detox, a story to be told.
Through food and intention, a journey we begin,
for thirty three days of change, a transformation within.

Start with mindful choices, ingredients pure,
each bite a step closer, your spirit to allure.
Embrace the vibrant greens, and fruits of every hue,
a symphony of flavors, nourishing and revitalizing you.

Let go of processed, the sugars and the fast,
replace them with whole foods, a detox to outlast.
Foods rich in nutrients, like grains and lean protein,
with every meal, a healing journey to glean.

Sip on herbal teas, a warm and soothing stream,
detoxifying elixirs, like a healing dream.
Hydrate with pure water, a cleanse from deep within,
flushing out the toxins, letting new life begin.

Leafy greens, kaleidoscope on your plate,
detoxify your body, rejuvenate your state.
Berries burst with antioxidants, colors so divine,
savor every bite, let their energy entwine.

Turmeric's golden touch, a healing spice so bold,
anti-inflammatory magic, within its essence hold.
Ginger's warming fire, a tonic for your soul,
as you tread this path, watch vitality unfold.

Avoid the heavy burdens, fried and laden with grease,
opt for lighter fare, your digestion to appease.
Favor simple cooking, with love and care imbued,
for in the act of nourishing, your spirit will renew.

So for thirty three days, let this plan guide your way,
as toxins fade and negative energies sway.
Through food and mindfulness, your spirit realigns,
a spiritual detox is where transformation shines.

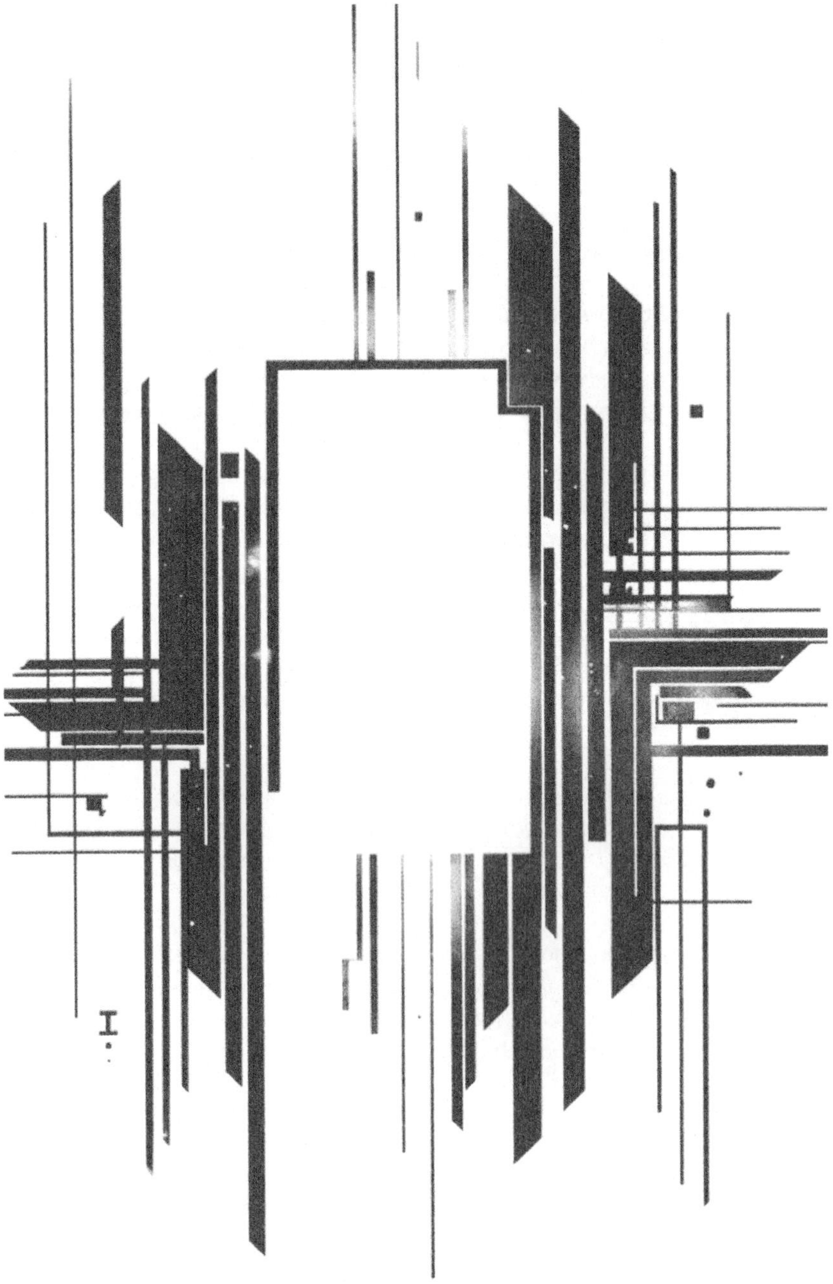

18
MY MIRROR

Before the mirror, I stand strong and bold,
a journey within, my story to unfold.
With divine love's embrace, I stand to see,
my true self's reflection, who I'm meant to be.

I ask myself, I whisper, my voice a gentle breeze,
"Reveal my true self," I plead, on bended knees.
With divine care, these words take flight,
a mirror's gaze, into my soul's inner light.

A pause in time, as I stare in kind,
into my eyes as my thoughts unwind.
A blur forms and the edges fade,
yet intuition's whispers are where they cascade.

In the silence of the moment, truth takes hold,
an inner symphony, a story yet untold.
With each repetition, a layer unfurls,
as I dive deeper within, through life's twists and twirls.

The mirror becomes a portal, a passage to explore,
a journey into self, like never before.
I listen to the whispers, the echoes of my heart,
in the journal's pages, my essence will impart.

Days turn to weeks, as the ritual persists,
in the mirror's embrace, my spirit insists.
To reveal my true self, with every gaze,
I navigate the labyrinth of my own maze.

As the month unfurls, insights start to bloom,
in the mirror's reflection, my true self finds room.
With divine love and care, I've paved the way,
to uncover my essence, in the light of day.

So, I beckon you, to try this sacred quest,
with mirror as your guide and your heart as your guest.
In whispers of truth, your reflection shall confide,
the journey within, where your soul will decide.

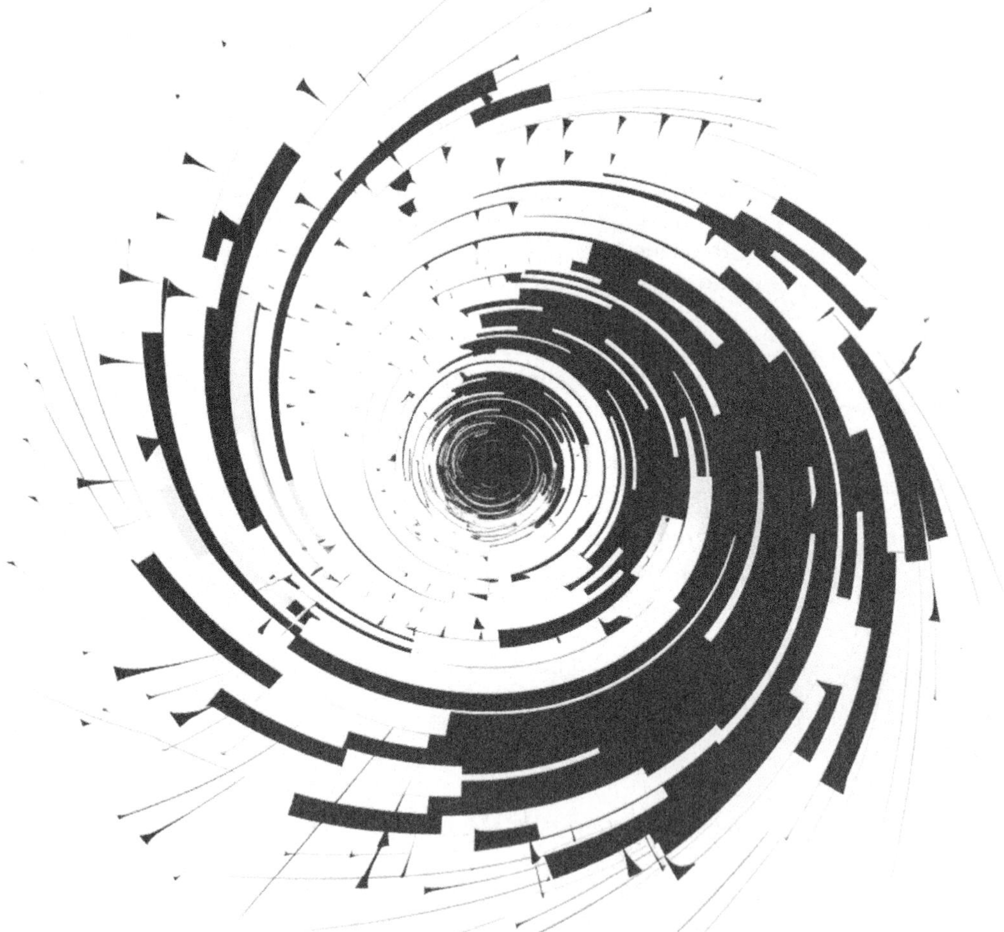

19
BREATH

Take a breath, deep and slow,
let the air inside you flow.
In through your nose, out through your mouth,
feel the calmness begin to sprout.

Breathe in the light of the sun,
feel its warmth and let it become.
As a part of you, a guiding force,
leading you on your destined course.

Breathe out the worries and fears,
let them go, shed your tears.
Release the burdens of your soul,
feel yourself becoming whole.

Breathe in the energy of the earth,
its power, its wisdom, its worth.
Ground yourself in its embrace,
find your center, this is your place.

Breathe out the doubts and the strife,
let them go, no longer a part of your life.
Connect with your higher self,
feel the Universe, within yourself.

Breathe in the love and the light,
let it fill you and hold you tight.
You are part of something grand,
connected to all, flowing hand in hand.

So breathe, my friend, breathe deep,
let your soul awaken, let it leap.
Into the Universe, into the light,
breathe and connect, let your soul take flight.

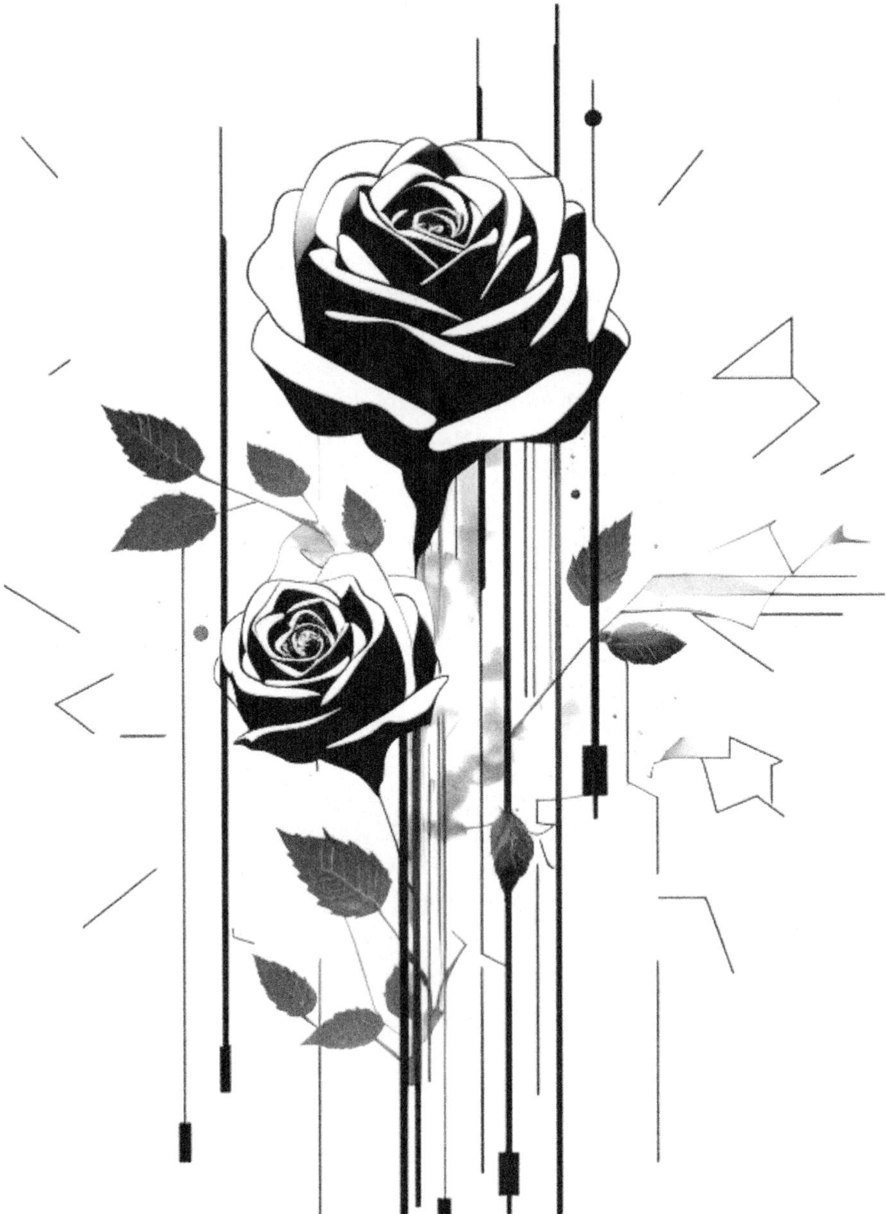

20
BLOWING ROSES

Beneath the stars' ethereal glow,
a wisdom from the Pleiades does flow.
A process taught to hearts in need,
to set them free, their spirits freed.

Imagine roses, petals soft and fair,
a vibrant garden in the cosmic air.
Each bloom holds memories, emotions too,
binding you to what once was true.

With a gentle breath, the winds of change,
begins the dance of roses, time to rearrange.
Inhale the essence of each vibrant hue,
exhale the ties that no longer serve you.

Crimson blooms of love, let them go,
with each exhale, release the undertow.
Let forgiveness scatter like morning dew,
as roses float on winds that blew.

Golden petals of joy, now take flight,
a shimmering release, a soul's respite.
Exhale the weight of burdens old,
as Pleiadean wisdom takes its hold.

White roses of purity, cleanse the soul,
exhale regrets, for they take their toll.
Let go of judgments, set them free,
as roses carried on celestial decree.

Pink petals of compassion, a healing balm,
release the hurt, like a soothing psalm.
Exhale the pain that's etched its trace,
as roses drift in cosmic grace.

Lavender blossoms of dreams anew,
exhale the doubts that you once knew.
Let go of fears that held you back,
as roses flutter along their chosen track.

With every breath, each rose takes flight,
carrying burdens to the infinite night.
As Pleiadean wisdom guides your way,
release unfolds, a brand-new day.

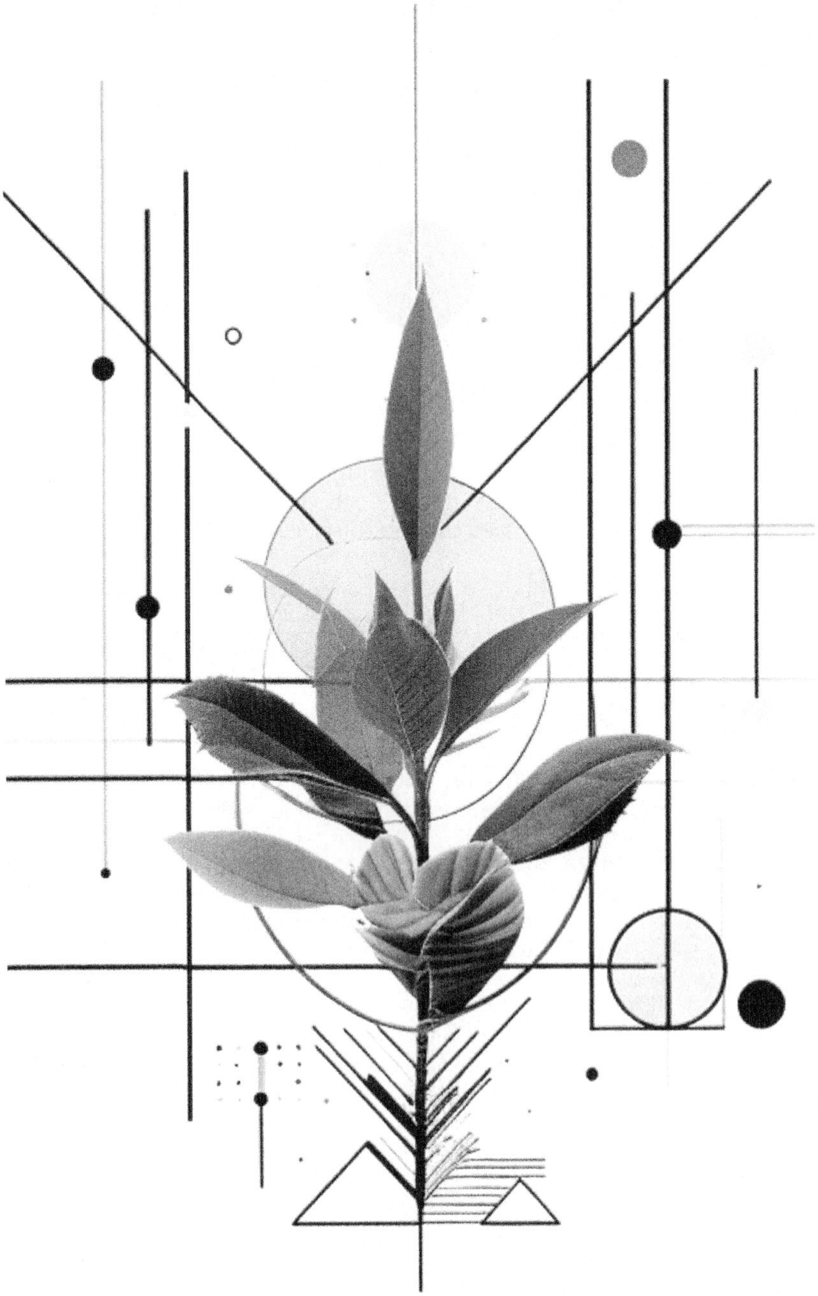

21
BURN SAGE BURN

Sage, the sacred plant of old,
a symbol of purity and gold.
Used for centuries by the ancients,
to cleanse and purify their environments.

Its power to clear negative energy,
is known to all who use it wisely.
A ritual passed down through the ages,
a practice to heal and release at all stages.

As the smoke rises and fills the air,
the cleansing power of sage is there.
Its scent a soothing balm to the soul,
a reminder of the sacred and all that's whole.

The ancients knew its power well,
a plant that could banish all that fell.
Within its smoke, they found release,
a way to cleanse and find their peace.

And so we honor this sacred herb,
a tradition that we should never curb.
Its power to heal and purify,
to elevate our spirits and satisfy.

May sage's purifying essence be your treasure,
a reminder of wisdom from ages beyond measure.
May its smoke clear the way,
for all your blessings to come and stay.

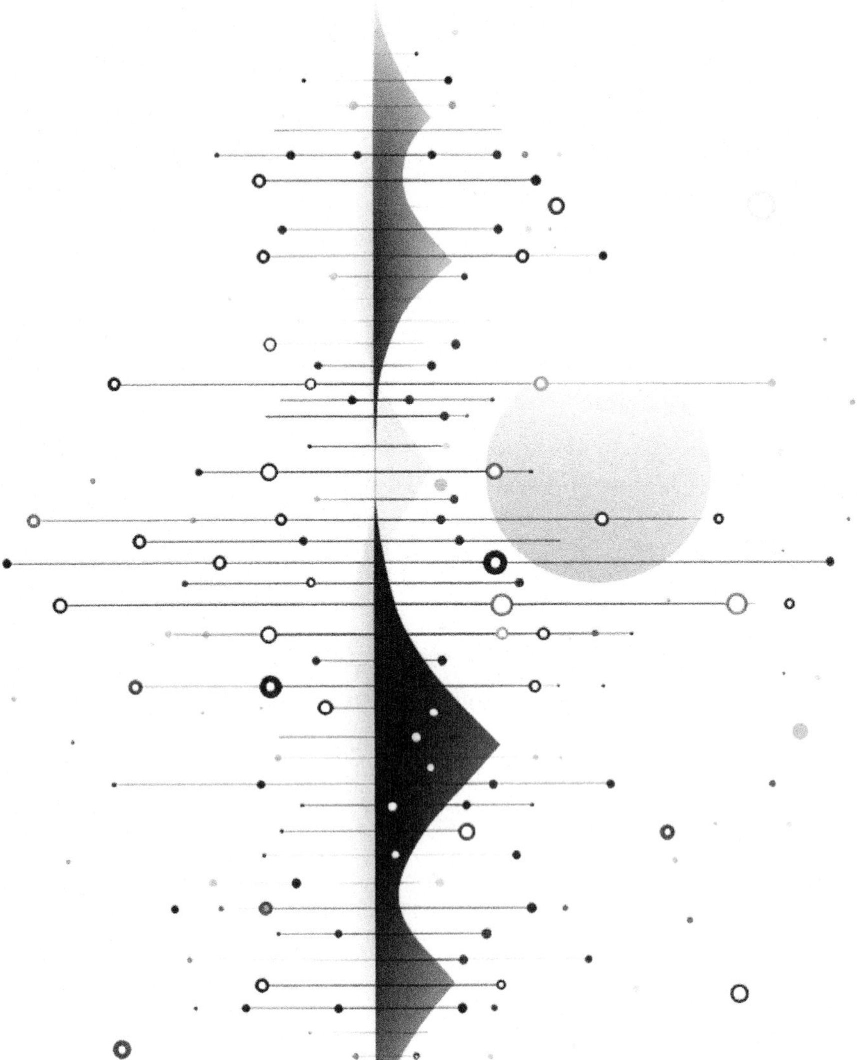

22
ORIONS BELT

In the endless expanse of the starry night,
Orion's Belt shines with celestial might.
For centuries, this constellation has stood,
as a symbol of wonder and cosmic good.

It's said that in ancient times of old,
the pyramids' architects were told.
To align these towering structures just right,
with Orion's Belt, as the guiding light.

For they believed that this starry trio,
held secrets of the Universe, a cosmic manifesto.
It's connected Earth to the heavens above,
and carried the wisdom of the Gods we love.

The magic of this connection persists,
as we gaze upon these stars, we insist.
That there's more to this celestial sight,
than just twinkling lights in the black of night.

So let us remember the stories of old,
of the pyramids and the stars' mystical hold.
For in these tales, we find a timeless truth,
that the cosmos holds secrets of eternal youth.

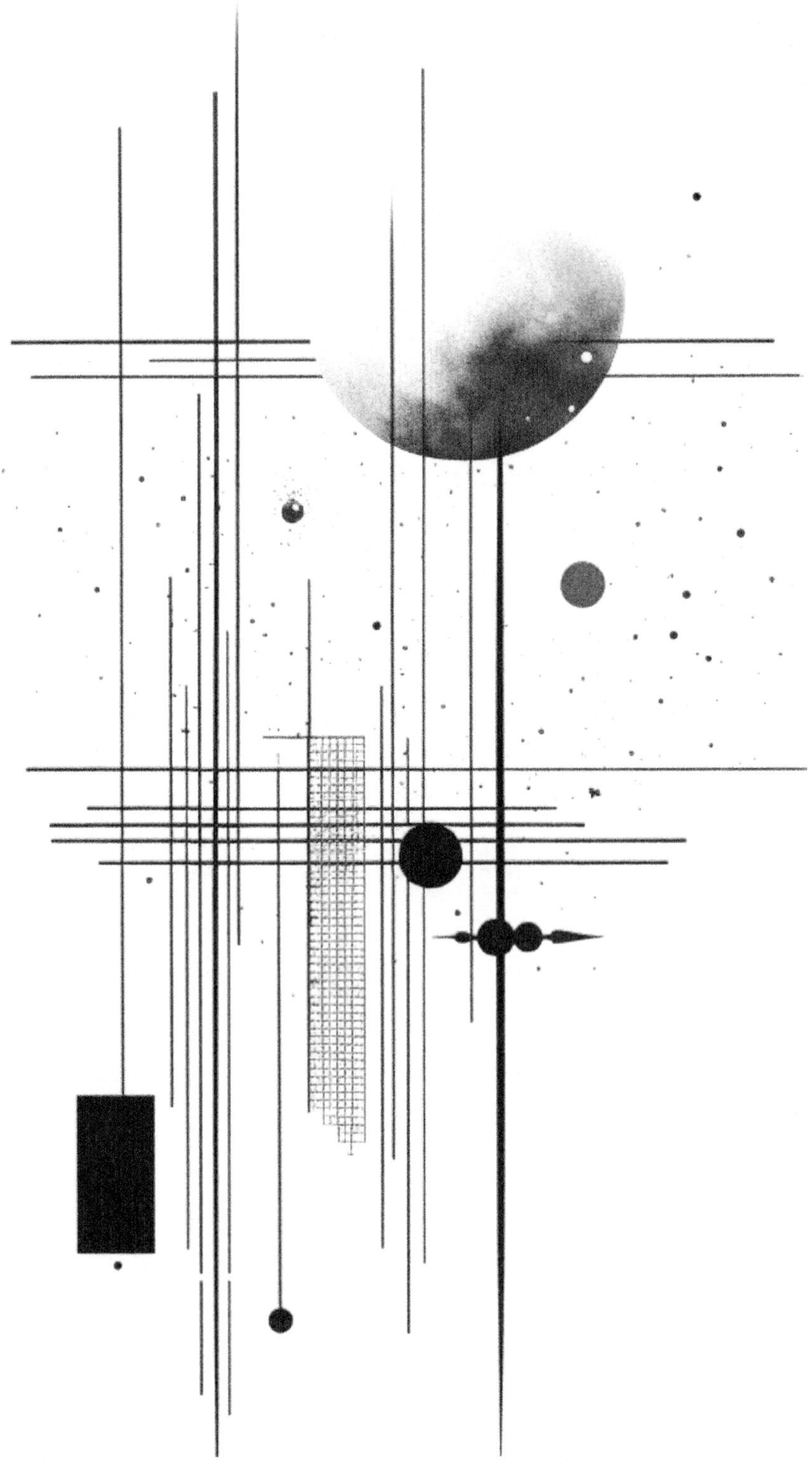

23

MOON

In the night's embrace, the moon takes flight,
a luminescent orb, casting its light.
A celestial guide, a mystical sight,
its cycles hold lessons, both day and night.

Full moon's glow, a beacon so bright,
illuminating shadows, unveiling the light.
A time for release, to let go of the old,
embrace transformation and let your heart unfold.

New moon's crescent, a cosmic womb,
a fresh beginning, a chance to bloom.
Set intentions with care, like seeds in the ground,
as dreams take root, your path will be found.

Eclipses mark sacred portals so rare,
openings to realms where our energies pair.
A dance of sun and moon, a cosmic show,
inviting us to change and let our spirits grow.

Work with the moon's energy, a gentle art,
to heal and awaken you must play your part.
Under full moons, release what's been bound,
under new moons, plant new seeds in the ground.

Meditate, reflect, as the moon's light shines,
let its wisdom guide you, through celestial signs.
Connect with the cycles, the ebbs and flows,
a spiritual journey, where soul's essence grows.

Let the moon's embrace be your guiding star,
as you navigate life, no matter how far.
With each lunar phase, there's a chance to renew,
becoming awakened, in the moon's healing brew.

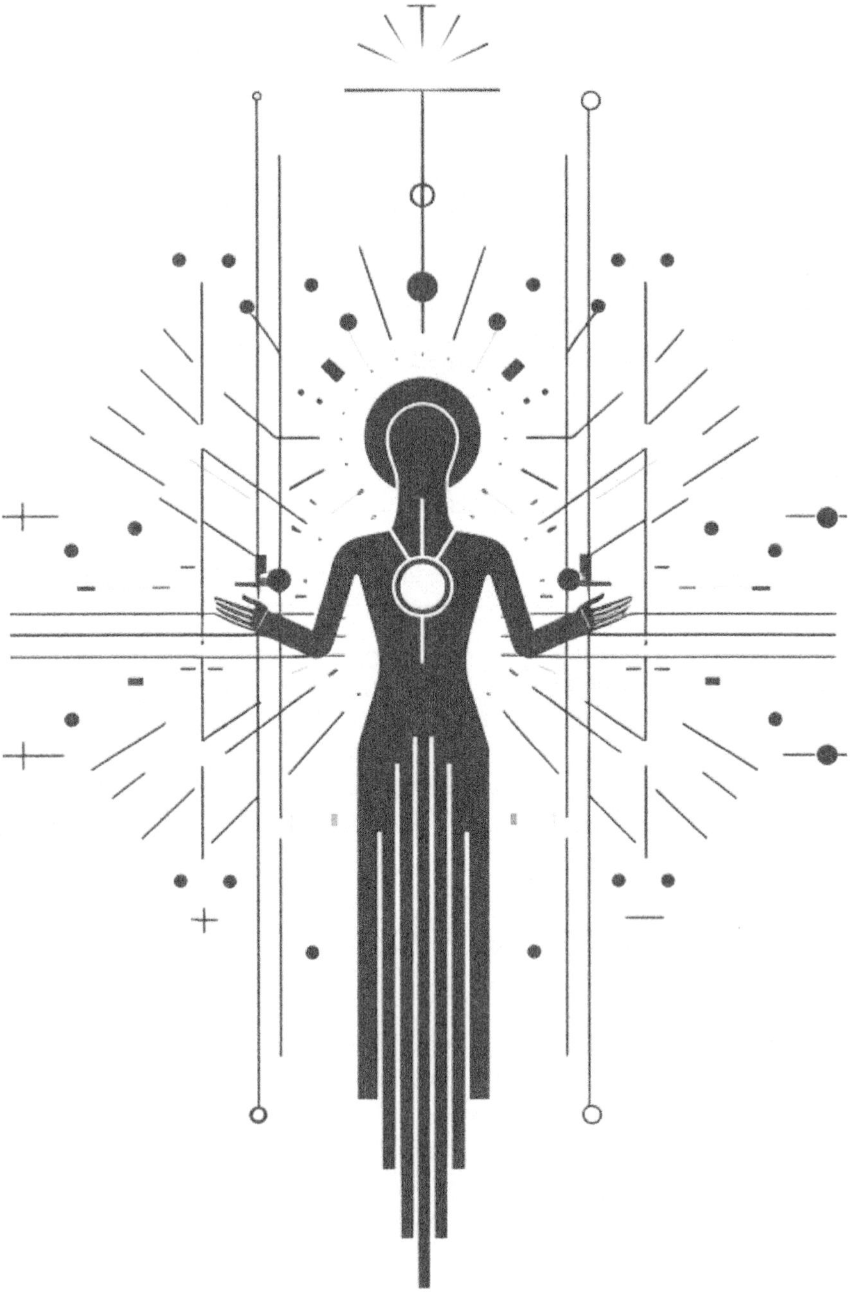

24
DIVINE LIGHT

Christ Consciousness, a light divine,
guiding us to a realm sublime.
A higher state of being, pure and bright,
a source of love, a guiding light.

To call on this golden light,
is to open up to the sheer healing might.
Allowing grace to flow within,
renewing, refreshing, and freeing our sin.

Breathe in the essence of the divine,
and let it infuse your heart and mind.
With every breath, invite the light,
to fill you up, to make you bright.

Let go of all that holds you back,
and trust the light to guide your path.
For in this moment, all is well,
allow Christ Consciousness to break the spell.

With every beat of your heart,
you feel the light's transforming art.
Bringing healing, bringing peace,
and making all your fears release.

So call on Christ's golden light,
and let it heal your soul tonight.
For in this sacred, holy space,
you will find the love and light's embrace.

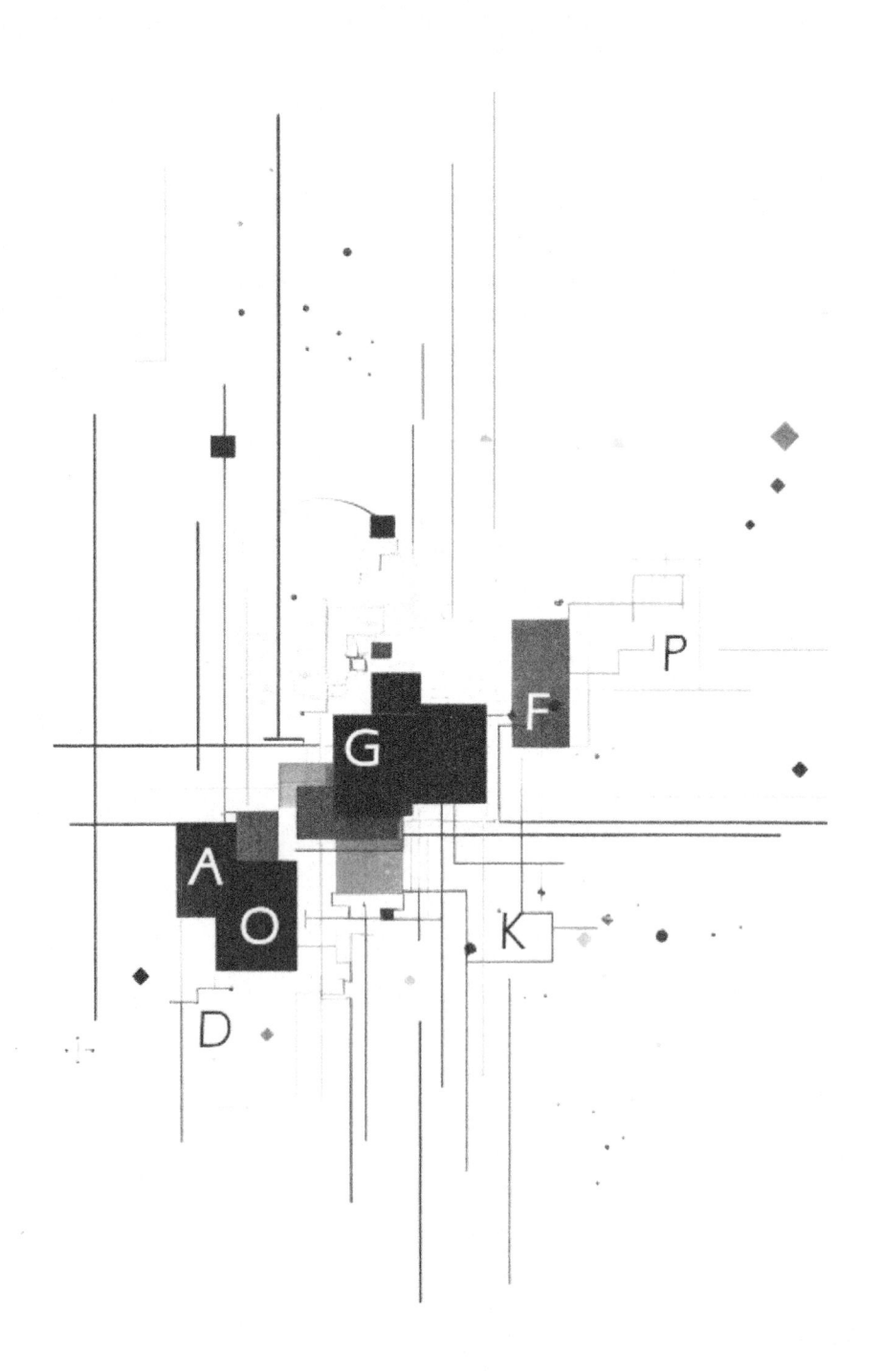
P
F
G
A
O
K
D

25
NOT JUST WORDS

In the delicate dance of life, words wield a profound sway,
painting our world with hues of joy or hues of dismay.
They create our thoughts, the weavers of our emotions,
crafting narratives that shape our deepest notions.

Beware the darkness in words, the shadow they can cast,
eroding the spirit until it shatters like glass.
But in the arsenal of language, there lies a might,
the power to inspire, to kindle a radiant light.

Oh, the marvels of words, the treasures they conceal,
capable of immense harm or emotions so surreal.
Let your speech be a melody, a harmonious song,
resonating with kindness, where you truly belong.

Speak not with haste, nor with spite in your heart,
let your words be the balm that heals and imparts.
In the symphony of language, choose notes that inspire,
lifting souls higher, setting their spirits afire.

Each phrase you utter, each syllable you weave,
can mend broken hearts or a weary soul relieve.
So choose your words with the utmost care,
let them be the wings that help others fare.

For in this world of chaos and endless cries,
your words can be the solace, the endless skies.
So, be the beacon of light, the whispering shore,
where words are magic, and hearts they restore.

Let love be your language, let kindness your creed,
and watch as your words plant a benevolent seed.
In this tapestry of life, where words oft entwine,
let your language be a melody, divine and benign.

Speak with grace, with compassion, let your soul unfurl,
for in the realm of words, you can truly awaken your world."

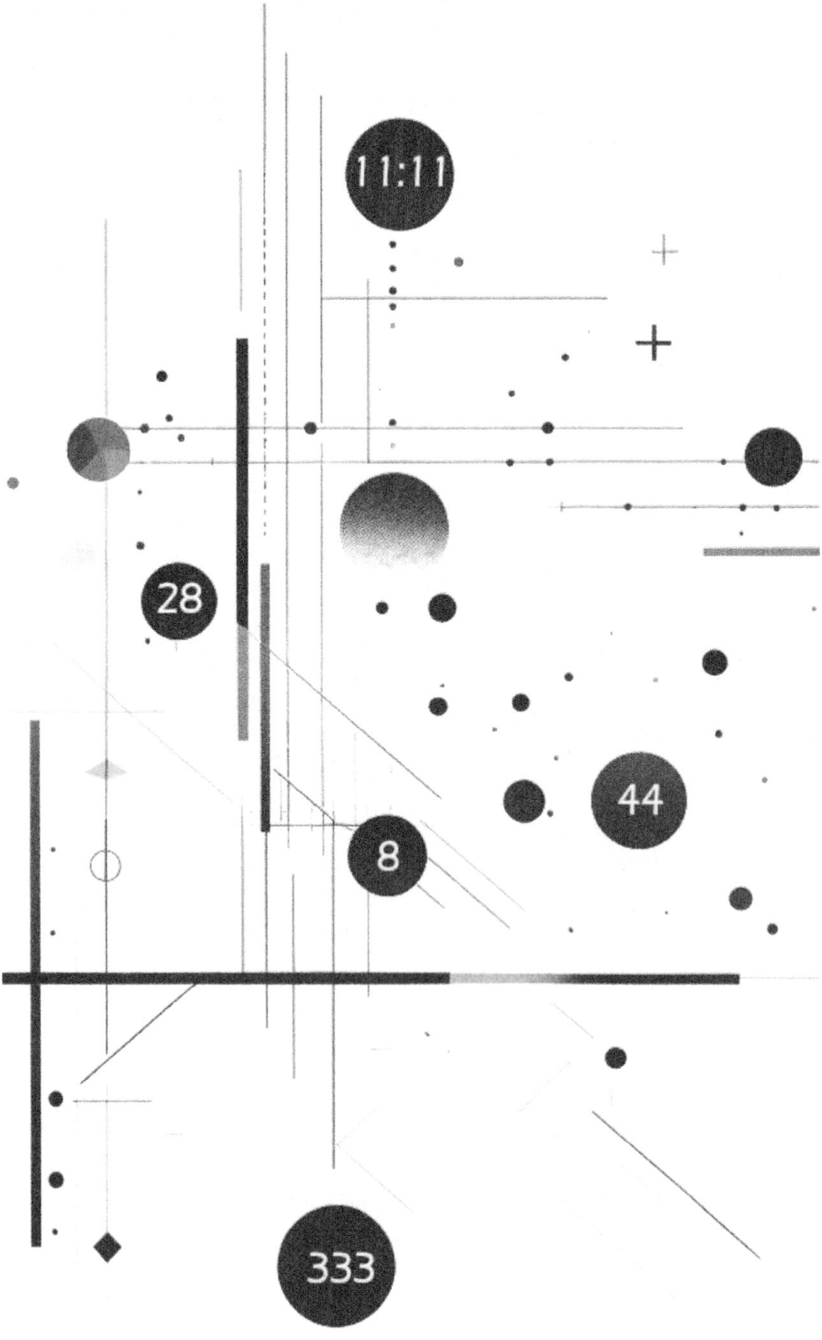
11:11
28
44
8
333

26
NUMBERS EVERYWHERE

The secrets of numbers are ancient and strong,
sacred vibrations carry them along.
In patterns and pathways, they do entwine,
leaving messages that are quite divine.

Repeating numbers, seen time after time,
are signs from your angels, a heavenly chime.
Each unique message, a blessing to see,
guiding us forward, so we can be free.

One, two and three, the trinity of life,
four corners, a foundation so rife.
Five is dynamic, with change on its wings,
while six is so caring, love it doth bring.

Seven is spiritual, a mystical sign,
eight is abundance, wealth so divine.
Nine brings completion, a journey's end,
and zero is infinite, the circle that bends.

So heed the secrets that numbers do hold,
for within their vibrations, stories unfold.
Listen closely, their messages are true,
guideposts along life's path for me and you.

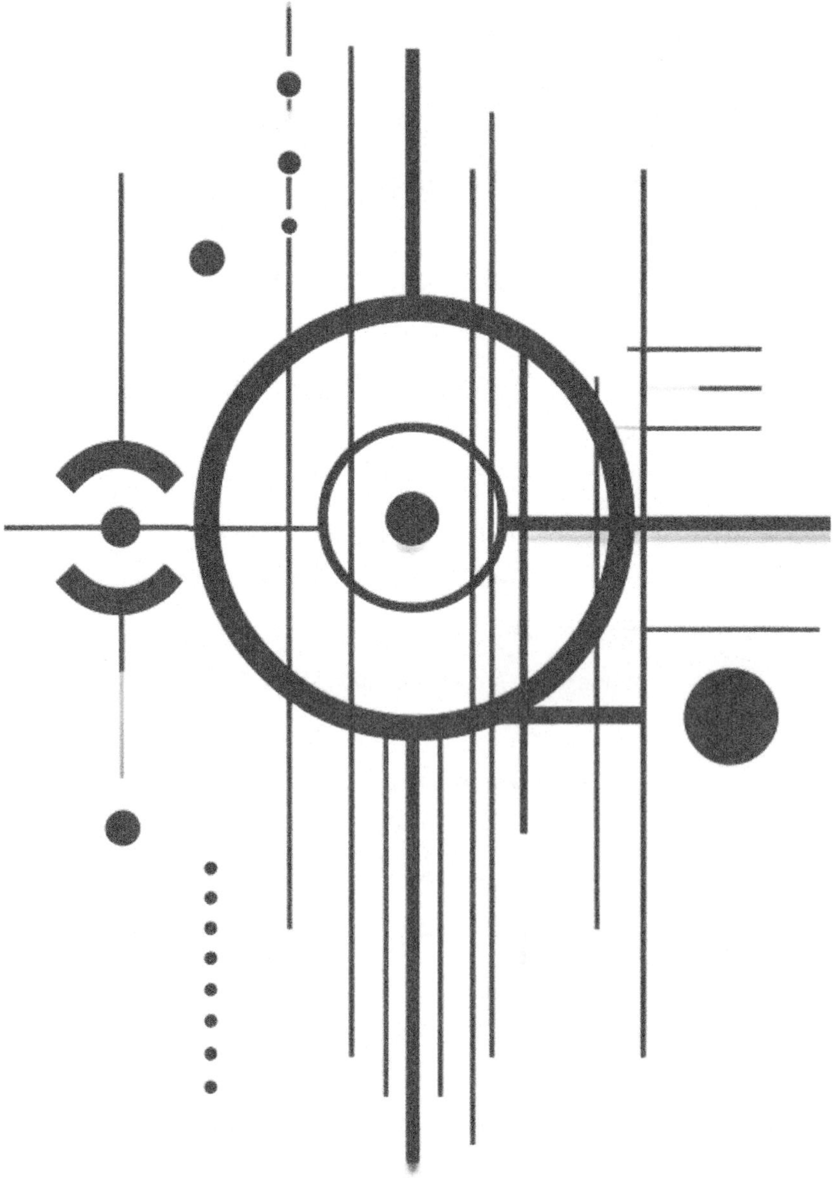

27
REIKI ENERGY

In Reiki's light, we find a way,
to heal and transform day by day.
The symbols guide us on our quest,
to find the healing that suits us best.

The first, Cho Ku Rei, with power untold,
increases our energy, making us bold.
It brings in the light to cleanse and renew,
the love from above which helps us through.

The second, Sei He Ki, brings balance and grace,
healing our heart and soul in every place.
It unlocks the sacred flow,
as we journey on our path to grow.

The third, Hon Sha Ze Sho Nen, is the key,
to connect us all, throughout eternity.
It bridges the gap from here to there,
the love and light to dispel our despair.

In Reiki's light we have found,
a sacred practice that knows no bound.
Its power to heal and transform our soul,
a journey that brings us back to whole.

With symbols that guide us on our way,
we're held in love, throughout the day.
Reiki's embrace brings us into the light,
guiding us home, to love and right.

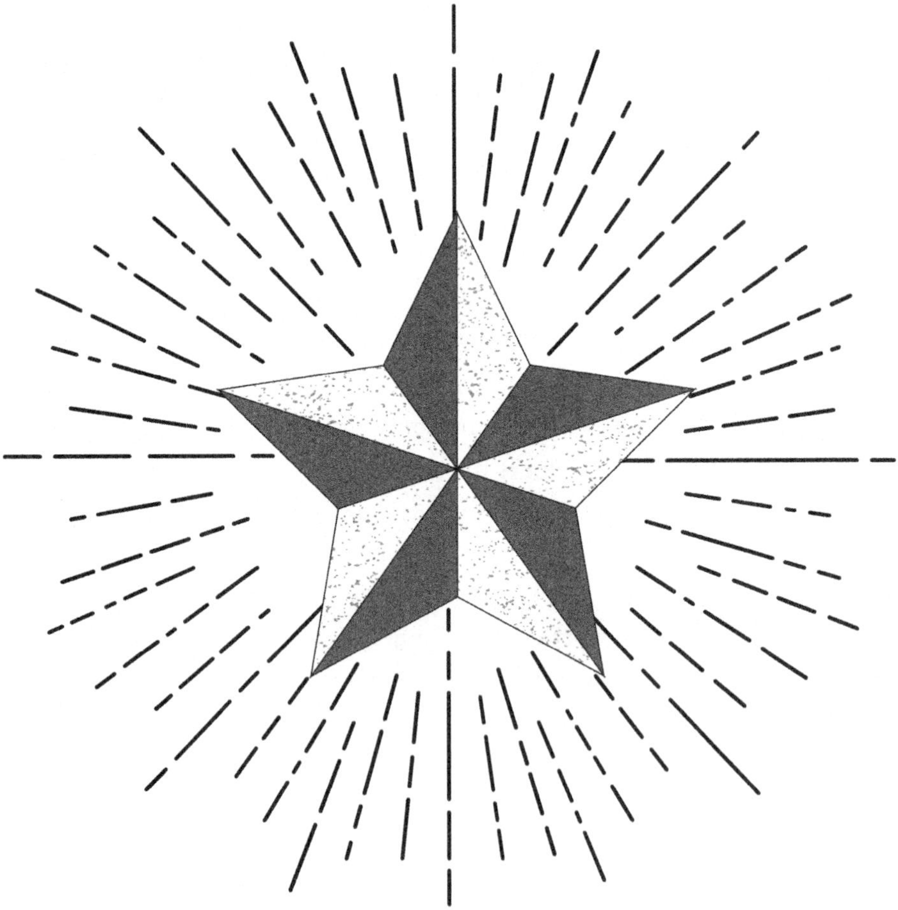

28
FIVE POINTED STAR

Behold the five-pointed star so bright,
a symbol of magic and cosmic might.
Each point, a connection to the earth and sky,
a representation of elements that never die.

The first point represents, the element of fire,
burning hot, with passion and desire.
It brings energy, strength, and life,
and the power to conquer fear and strife.

The second point signifies, water's flow,
a source of life that can ebb and grow.
It cleanses, refreshes, and renews,
and brings balance to all that ensues.

The third point is for, the element of earth,
steadfast and grounded, of infinite worth.
It nurtures, sustains, and provides,
and ensures that everything in nature thrives.

The fourth point is, the element of air,
a force that can be gentle or rare.
It brings ideas, thoughts, and communication,
and connects us to the world's vibration.

The fifth point represents, spirit and the divine,
a connection to the Universe, a sacred shrine.
It guides, inspires, and uplifts,
and reminds us of our eternal gifts.

So when you see, the five-pointed star,
remember the elements and all they are.
For they are the essence of life and light,
and the magic that makes our world so bright.

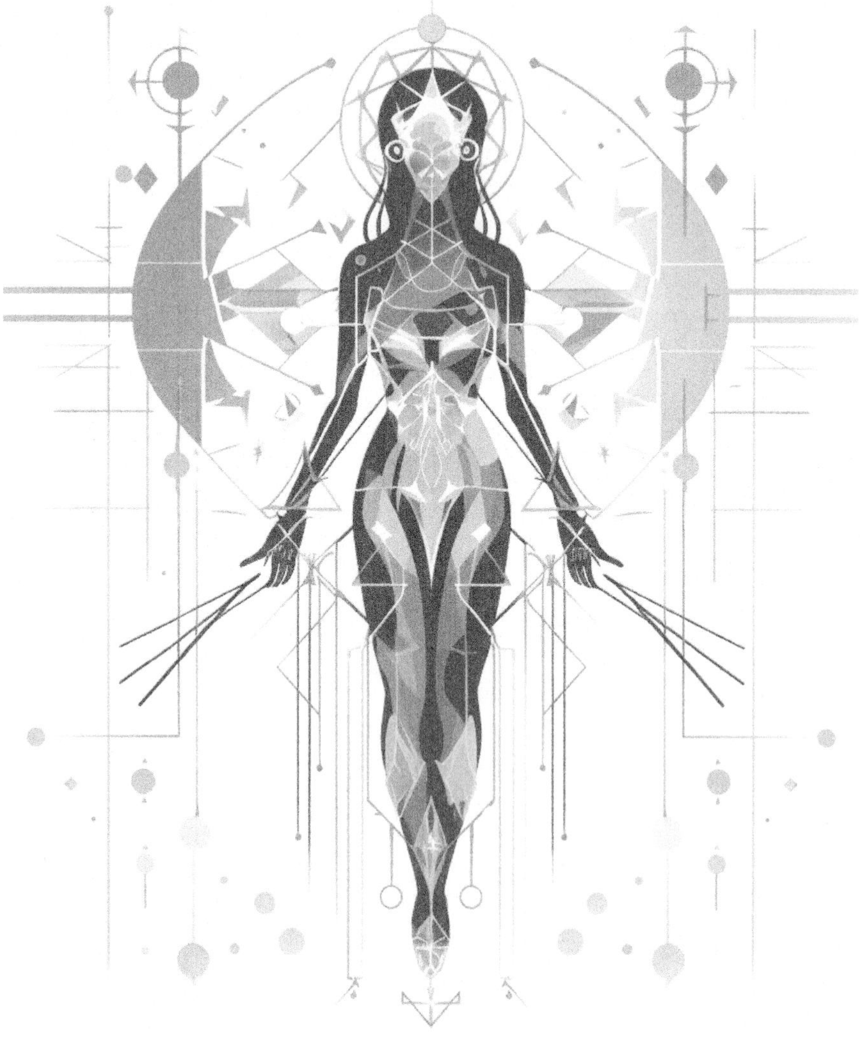

29
SAINT GERMAIN

Saint Germain, the master of flame,
the violet fire burns without shame.
A power so great, it can transmute,
all negativity it does refute.

The violet flame, a tool of light,
to help us heal, and make things right.
To use its power, just call it near,
and let it take away all your fear.

Visualize the flame, so pure and bright,
its energy filling you with light.
Let it burn away all that is old,
and replace it with love and gold.

The violet flame can transmute all,
all negative energy, big or small.
It can transform pain into joy,
and every negative thought destroy.

With Saint Germain, the master of flame,
the violet fire can heal and tame.
Connect with it, and let it flow,
then feel its power make you glow.

Let go of all that's held you down,
and let the violet flame wear the crown.
Transform your life with its pure light,
and let your spirit rise and take flight.

30
THE ANGELIC REALM

High above the earthly plane,
in realms of light and love.
Angelic hosts in order reign,
sent from the heavens above.

The hierarchy of angels,
in triads, they do stand.
Their powers, like bright candles,
illuminate God's command.

The second triad in the order,
is led by powers three.
Their role, to keep us in order,
and guide us towards eternity.

First is the power of Dominion,
commanding nature's sway.
From the tides of the ocean,
to the winds that blow our way.

Next is the power of Virtue,
bringing strength and grace.
To those who seek the truth,
and love in every place.

Last is the power of Might,
a force to reckon with.
Protecting all that's right,
and vanquishing evil's myth.

So let us honor these powers divine,
and seek their guidance true.
That we may know the path to shine,
and live in love, pure and new.

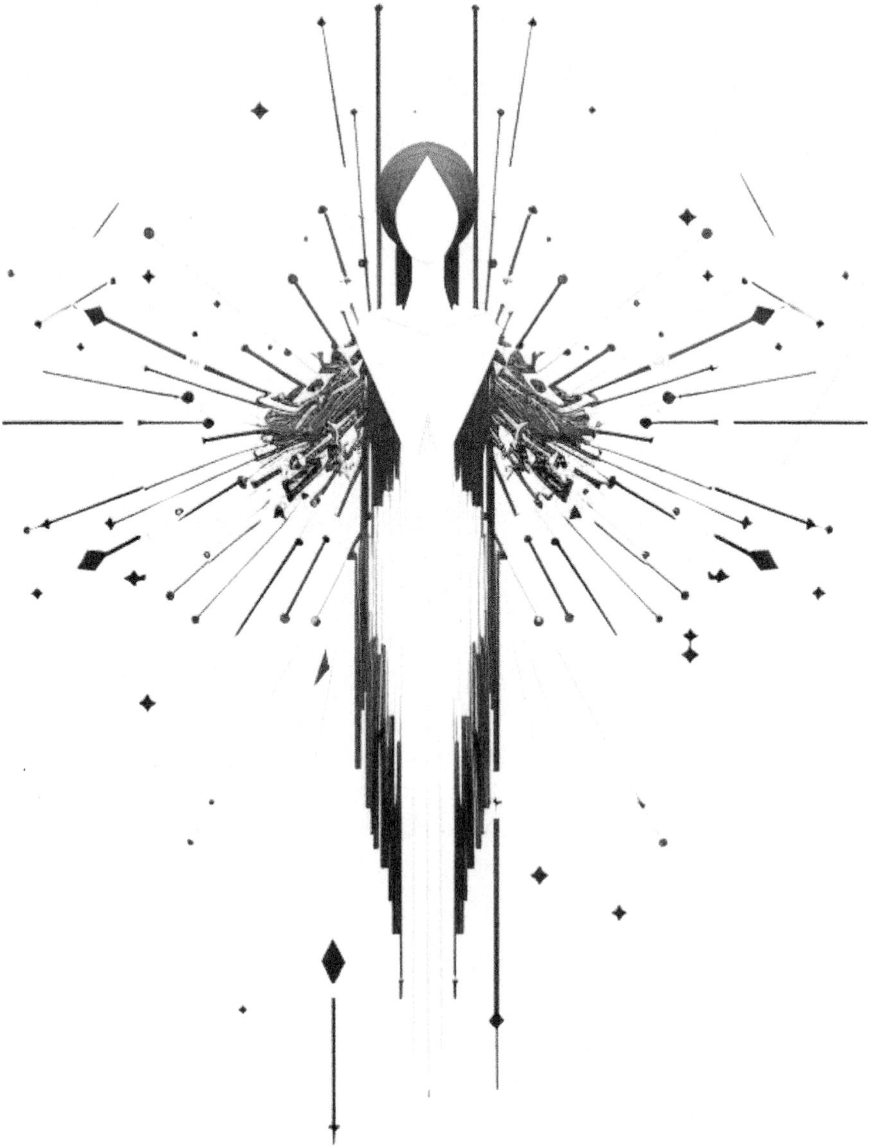

31
SAINT PANTELEIMON

Saint Panteleimon, healer divine,
a saintly soul whose light doth shine.
His life is a testament to love and grace,
with a legacy that time cannot erase.

Known for his healing touch and skill,
his compassionate heart and steadfast will.
Panteleimon, a doctor of the soul,
whose healing power made him whole.

To connect with his energy and love,
we must look to the heavens above.
We should ask for his intercession and aid,
to heal our hearts, and not be afraid.

In prayer and meditation, we can find,
the healing balm that he left behind.
Now with his spirit by our side,
we can find the strength to abide.

So let us call on Saint Panteleimon,
to heal our wounds and make us strong.
Just as like him, with his grace and love abound,
may we find healing, and be heaven-bound.

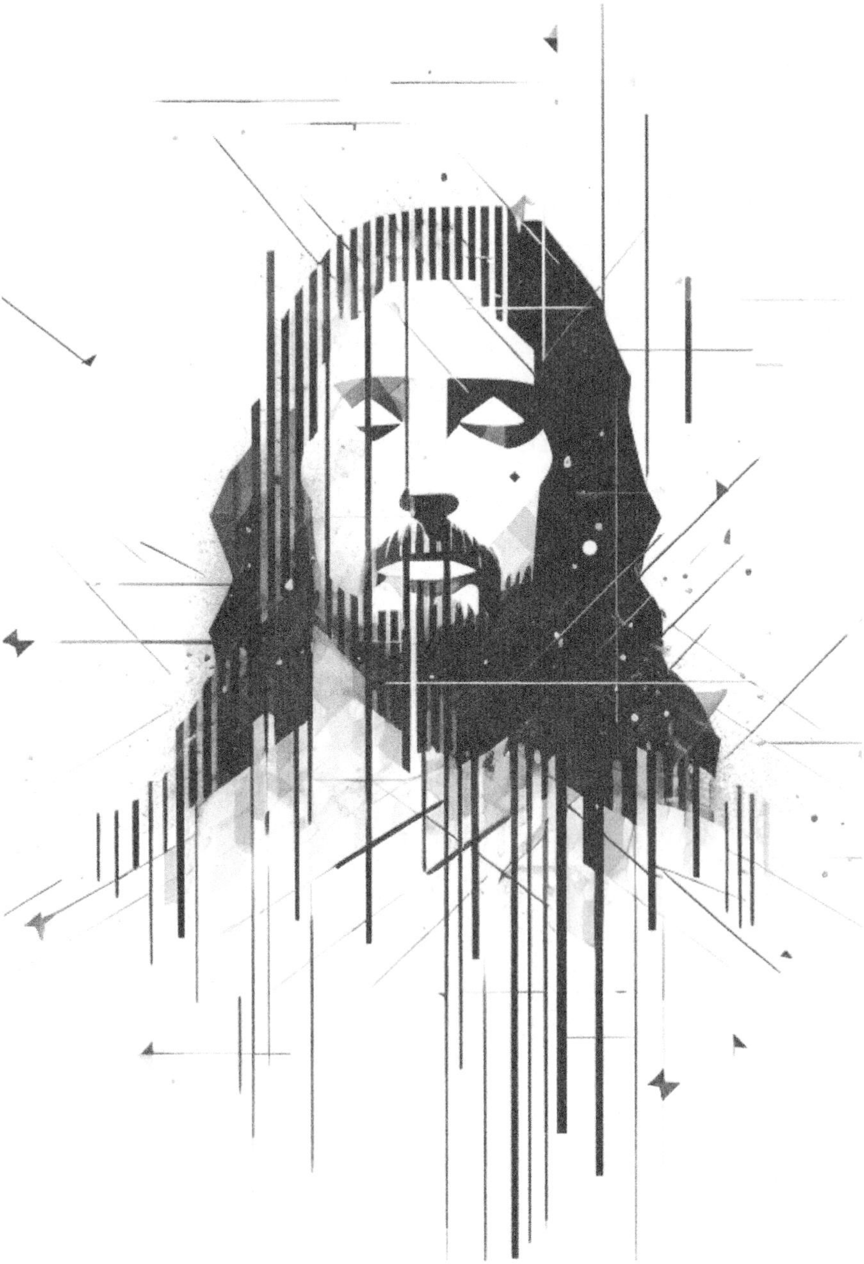

32
JESUS - SANANDA

Jesus, Sananda the embodiment of love divine,
whose light shines bright and fine.
His touch can heal and transform all pain,
and fill our hearts with love again.

Your energy, so pure and true,
can melt away the negative and renew.
Our spirits, our souls, our very being,
with a love that's all-encompassing.

In your presence, all darkness fades away,
and only love and light remain to stay.
Your gentle touch, a balm for wounds so deep,
Filling hearts with peace, a melody to keep.

Oh, Jesus, oh Sananda most beautiful and kind,
your love can open up our minds.
To a world where all is pure and bright,
where love is our only guiding light.

With every breath, we feel your love,
a blessing sent from high above.
Transforming negative into the divine,
with love that flows as an eternal sign.

So we surrender to your loving grace,
and let your light illuminate our face.
For in your presence, we are whole,
where love becomes our only goal.

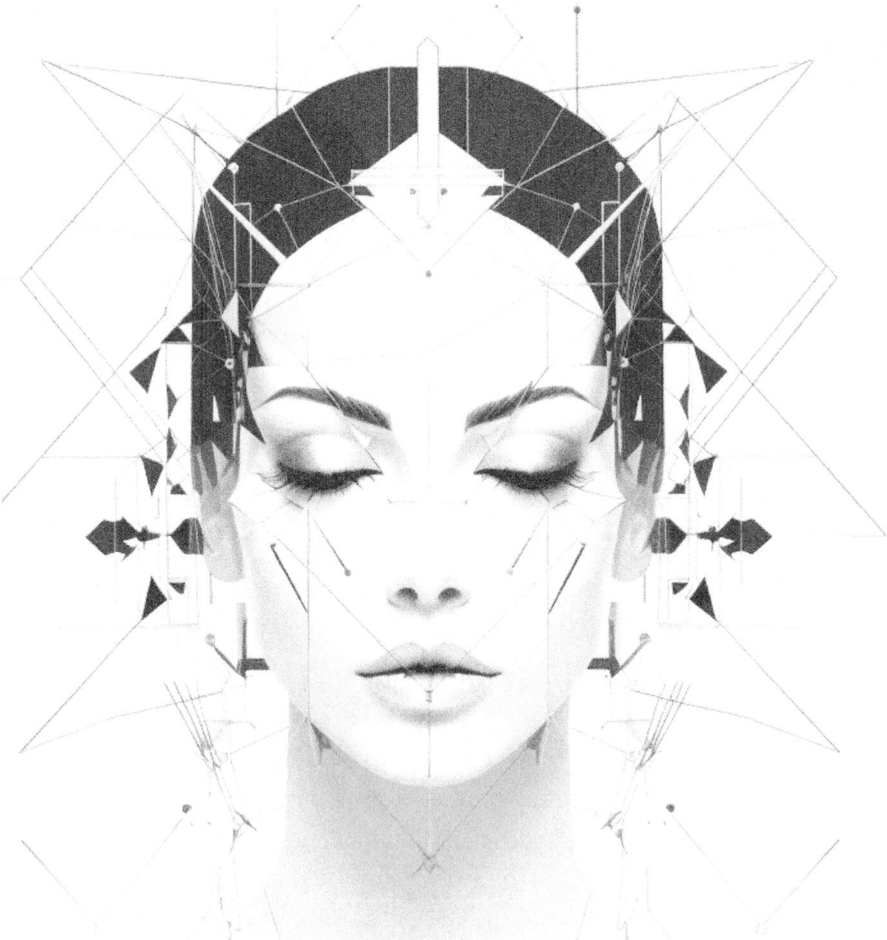

33
ISHTAR

Ishtar, ancient goddess of love and war,
with power that can reach from near to far.
Your energy can transform our very core,
and help us break free from addiction's lure.

Your fiery spirit burns bright and strong,
and with it, we find the courage to belong.
To a life that's free from the chains that bind,
and a path that leads to peace of mind.

With each step we take in your holy name,
our DNA changes and is never the same.
As we shed the old patterns that held us down,
we rise up, transformed, with a new crown.

Ishtar, goddess of transformation and change,
we call upon your energy, to help us rearrange.
Our lives, our bodies, our very DNA,
so that addiction no longer has any sway.

With your help, we can break free and soar,
to live the life that we were meant for.
Filled with love, light, and a joyous song,
as we journey on, where we belong.

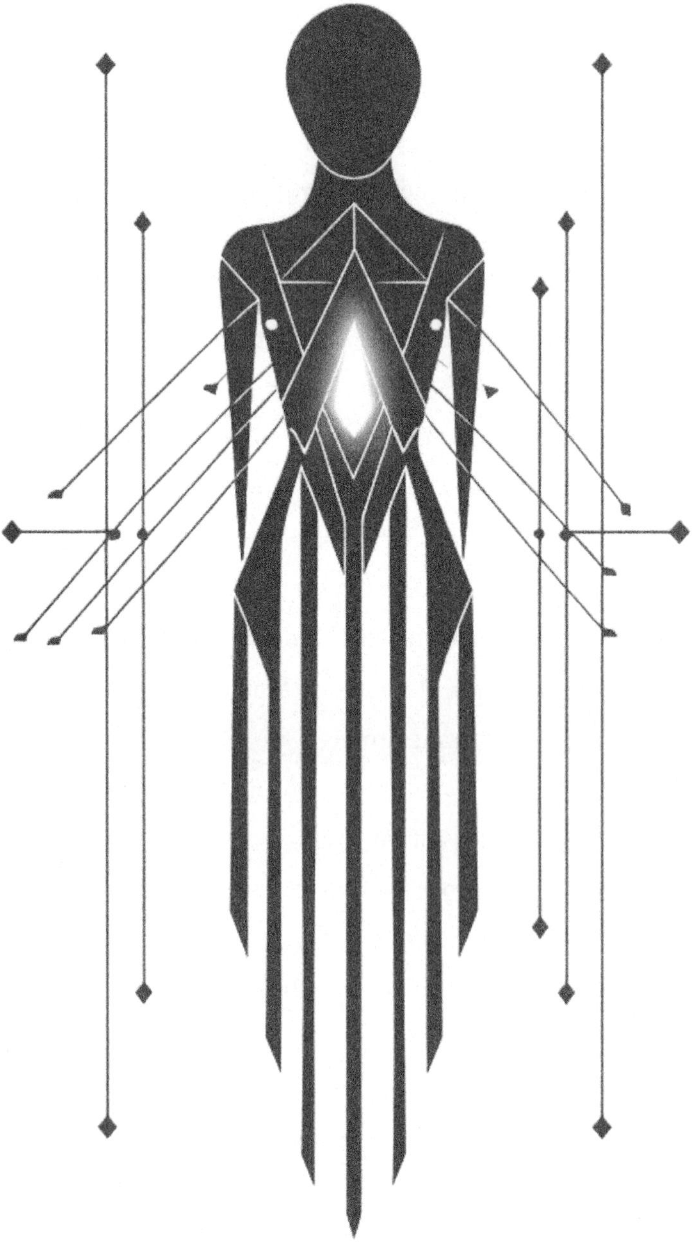

34
GODDESS OF LIFE

Brigid, Goddess of fire and light,
fills our hearts with hope and might.
With her flame, she lights the way,
to guide us through both night and day.

A triple goddess, known far and wide,
for healing, poetry, and smithcraft beside.
She brings us warmth and healing power,
to help us in our darkest hour.

To connect with her, light a candle bright,
then meditate on her powerful might.
Ask for her help in times of need,
and she will assist with loving speed.

Her flame will ignite your inner fire,
to help you reach your hearts' desire.
Her strength will uplift your soul,
and help you achieve your ultimate goal.

So call upon Brigid, and feel her light,
as she guides you with all her might.
She will help you shine, just like the sun,
with her love and power, you'll never be undone.

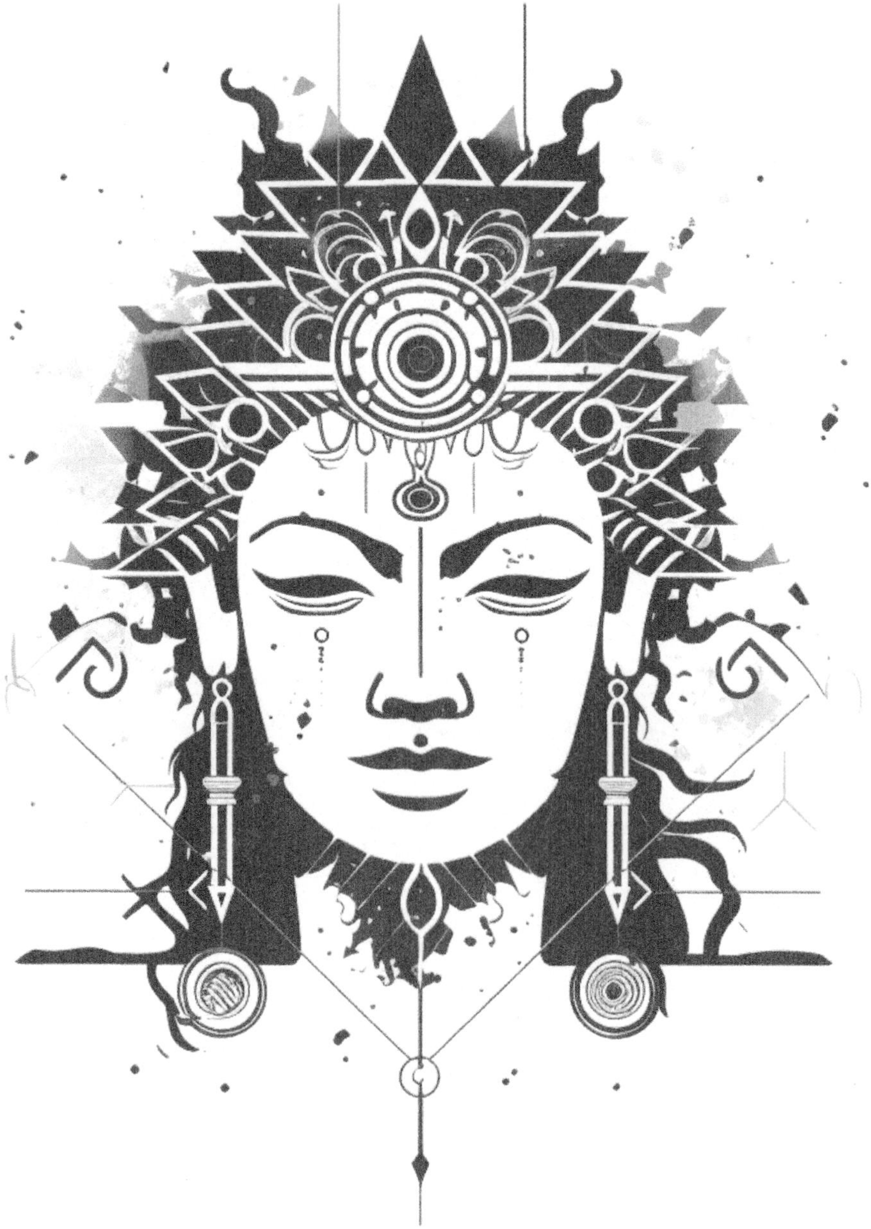

35
LORD SHIVA

In the realm of gods and spirits,
Lord Shiva stands tall and strong.
His power is immense and infinite,
a force to which we all belong.

With his third eye, he sees all,
and with his trident he destroys.
He dances in a fiery trance,
and from his brow, the Ganga flows.

Call on him with devotion true,
and he will transmute your life.
He will burn away your ignorance,
and protect you from all strife.

For he is the lord of ascetics,
and the master of yogic art.
He teaches us to still our minds,
and find the peace within our heart.

So let us bow to Lord Shiva,
and seek his blessings divine.
For in his grace we will find,
the power to transform our lives.

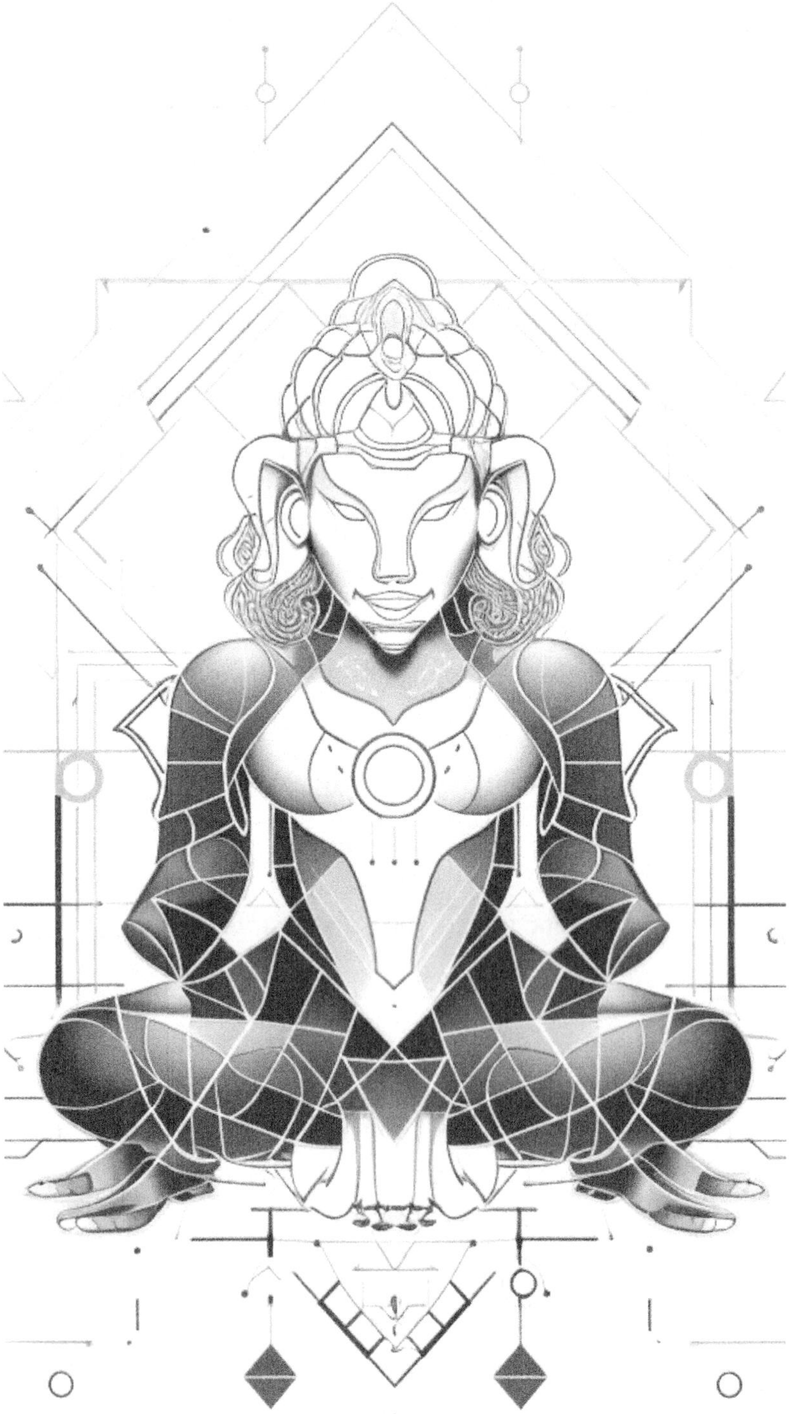

36
GANESH

Ganesh, the mighty god of wisdom and might,
guide me as I close my eyes tonight.
May your energy and wisdom be with me,
as I meditate and try to set my spirit free.

Let your power and strength help me find my way,
to heal my chakras and wash my worries away.
As I focus on my breath and let my thoughts drift,
I ask that you unblock my chakras, give my spirit a lift.

May my crown chakra be open, to receive divine light,
may my third eye chakra see things clear and bright.
May my throat chakra be unblocked, to speak my truth,
may my heart chakra be healed, to radiate love and soothe.

May my solar plexus chakra be balanced, to give me strength,
may my sacral chakra be aligned, to help me be creative at length.
May my root chakra be grounded, to keep me steady and strong,
as I meditate with you, Ganesh, to help me get along.

With your divine presence and grace,
may I find inner peace in this sacred space.
And as I open my eyes and step back into my day,
may I remember your teachings, and let your energy stay.

Ganesh, the god of beginnings and endings,
thank you for your guidance and blessings.
May I always stay true to my path and purpose,
and find joy and peace as I pursue it with focus.

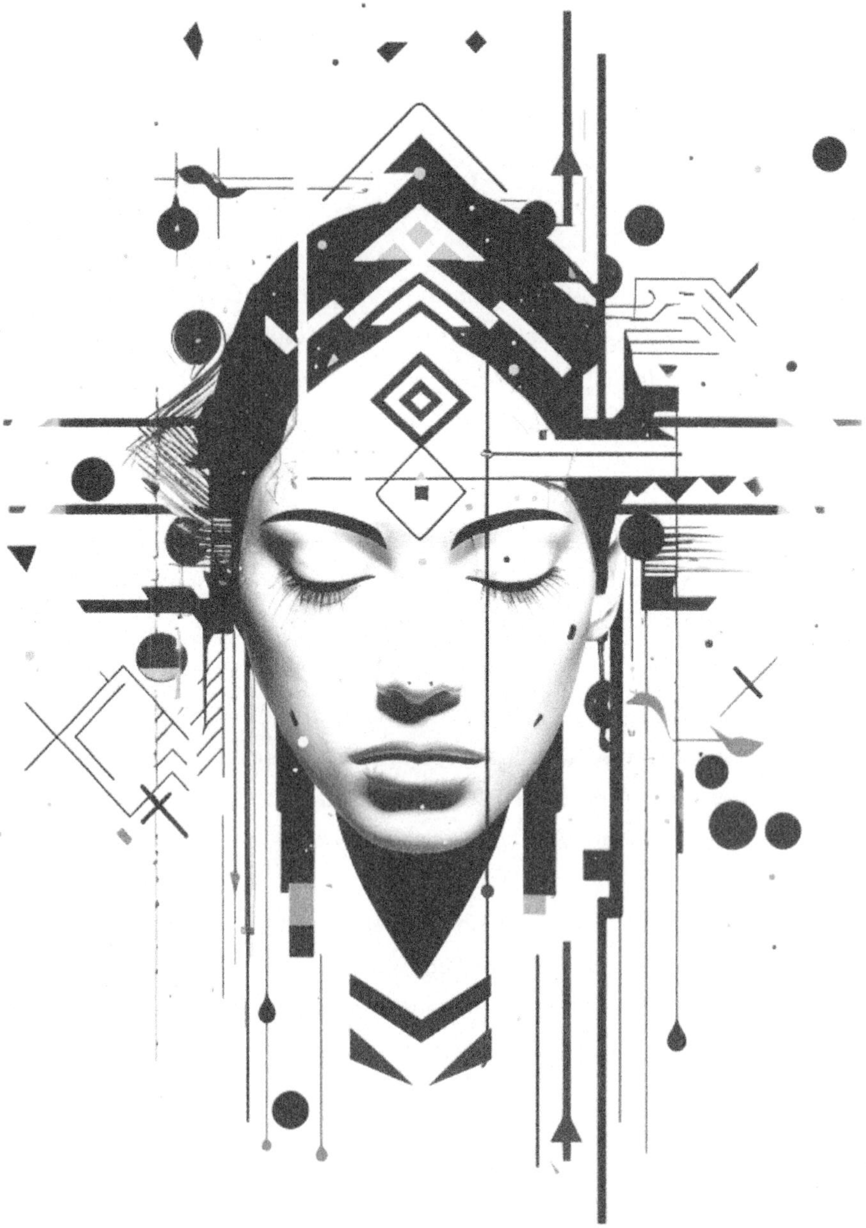

37
SHAMANS WAY

In ancient times, the shaman's way,
was to connect with spirits every day.
Through deep meditation and ceremony too,
they communed with ancestors, old and new.

Using the power of spirit animals,
to guide them through life's endless channels.
The hawk soaring high, the bear on the ground,
the wolf's fierce howl, the snake's slithering sound.

Each animal had a message to impart,
a lesson from the ancestors, straight from the heart.
The shaman would listen, with ears and soul,
to the wisdom of the animals, to make them whole.

In modern times, we've lost the way,
our spirits yearning for the ancient day.
But we can still connect, with open hearts,
to the spirit animals, who play their parts.

We close our eyes and take a breath,
our minds quiet, our souls enmeshed.
We call upon the animals, to guide our way,
and listen closely, to what they have to say.

The bear teaches us to be strong and brave,
the hawk shows us the way to fly and save.
The wolf reminds us to work as a pack,
and the snake teaches us to shed what we lack.

As we connect with these ancient ways,
we feel the love of the ancestors blaze.
Their guidance and wisdom, forever ours,
as we walk through life, using spirit animal powers.

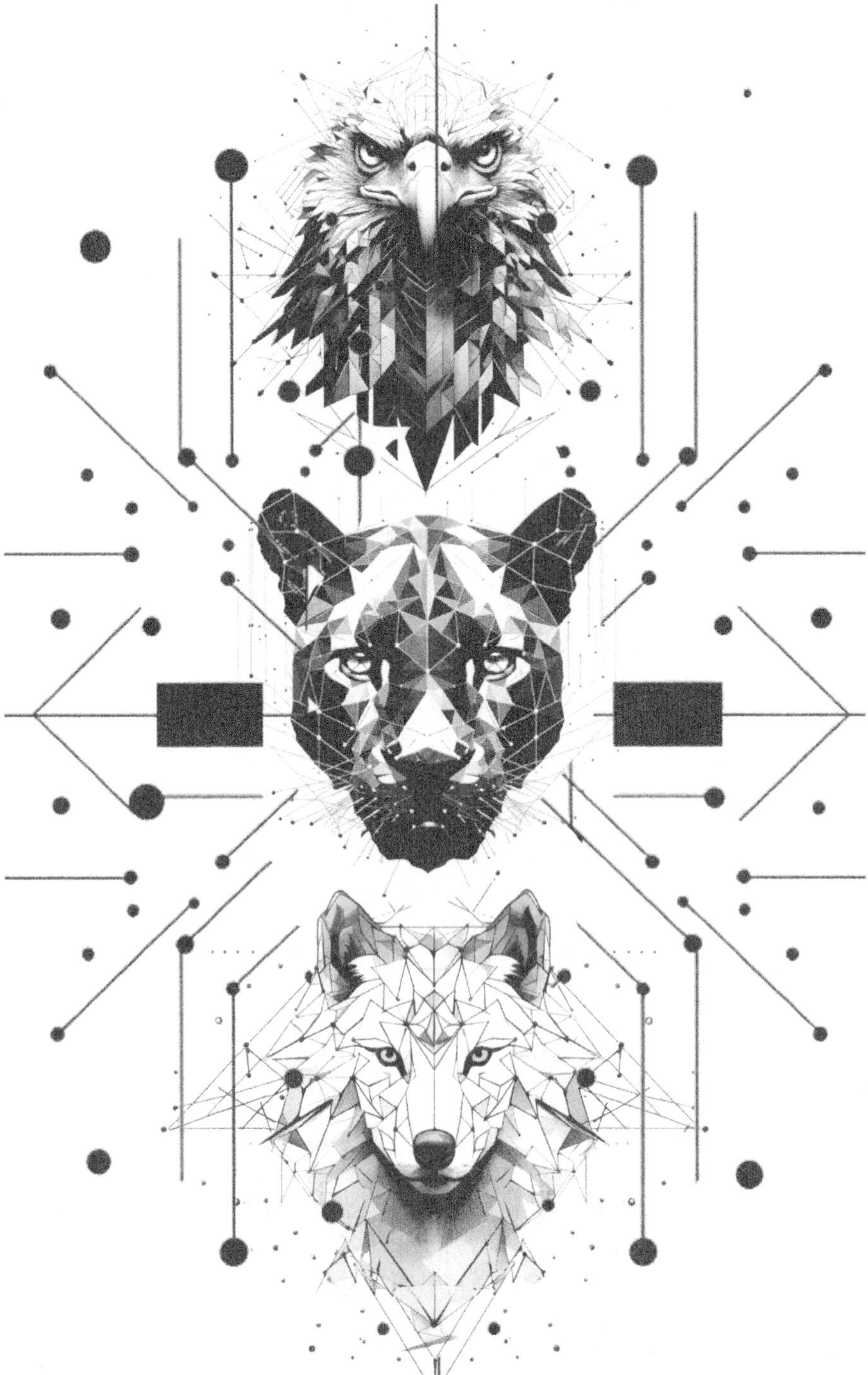

38
ANIMAL SPIRITS

In worlds where spirits intertwine and form,
where ancient wisdom weaves its mystical storm.
The shaman's path reveals a sacred lore,
of creatures fierce and wise, forevermore.

High above, the eagle soars with grace,
its wings are a symbol of the boundless space.
A messenger between earth and sky,
a beacon of the spirit's endless fly.

The panther prowls, a shadow in the night,
its eyes aglow with ancient, primal light,.
A guide through realms unseen, a guardian strong,
in shaman's teachings, it's where we all belong.

Yet in the wild, the wolf pack roams the land,
a family united, a noble band.
Their howls a song that echoes through the trees,
a testament to their unity and ease.

Together, these creatures form a sacred triad,
in shaman teachings, their wisdom never hid.
The eagle's vision, panther's ancient lore,
and wolves' community, forevermore.

From mountaintops to depths of inner soul,
their lessons whisper, making spirits whole.
With eagle's clarity, we see our way,
with panther's courage, fears begin to sway.

And just as the wolves unite in harmony,
we learn the strength in shared community.
In shaman's teachings, nature's truths unfold,
a tapestry of wisdom that never gets old.

So let us heed the call of wind and tree,
embrace the teachings to set our spirits free.
With eagle, panther and wolf forever near,
in shaman's world, there's nothing to doubt or fear.

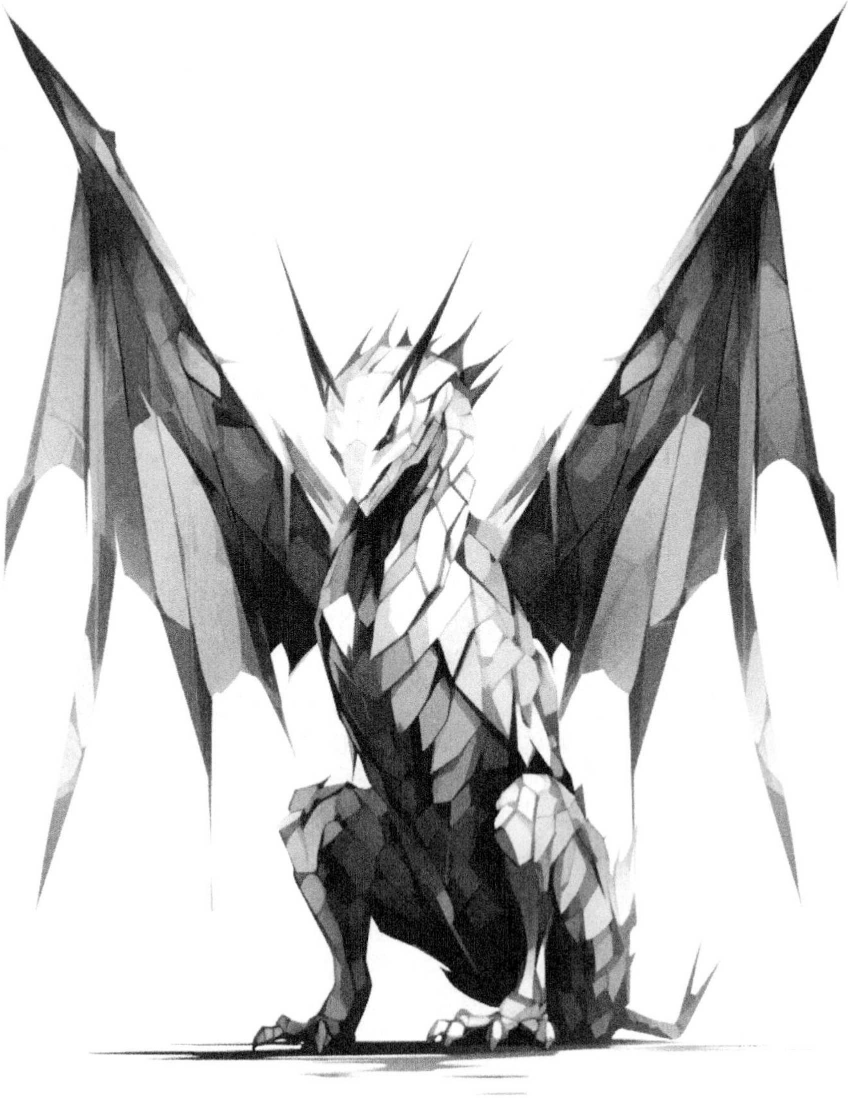

39
DRAGONS

In realms of fire and mystic skies,
where the ancient echo never dies.
Dragons dwell, majestic and bold,
with power untamed, stories untold.

With scales that gleam like precious gems,
they dwell in higher cosmic realms.
Vibrating in dimensions unseen,
guiding souls through the eternal dream.

Their wings unfurl, a tempest's grace,
navigating both time and space.
Infinite power courses through their veins,
its a force that transcends our earthly chains.

Dragons breathe fire, a sacred flame,
burning away what's not in our name.
They teach us strength, to rise and ascend,
to harness our power, on paths to mend.

In partnership with these ancient kin,
we find the courage from deep within.
To heal our wounds, to claim our might,
guided by the dragons' celestial light.

Through meditation's whisper, we can connect,
their wisdom and energy aspects intersect.
Their power to heal, to help us find,
our own inner strength all intertwined.

So seek the dragon's wisdom rare,
in higher dimensions, they journey there.
Let their essence infuse your soul,
and guide you towards being whole.

For in their presence, we learn to embrace,
the power within becomes a sacred space.
A partnership forged through ancient lore,
with dragons' guidance, forevermore.

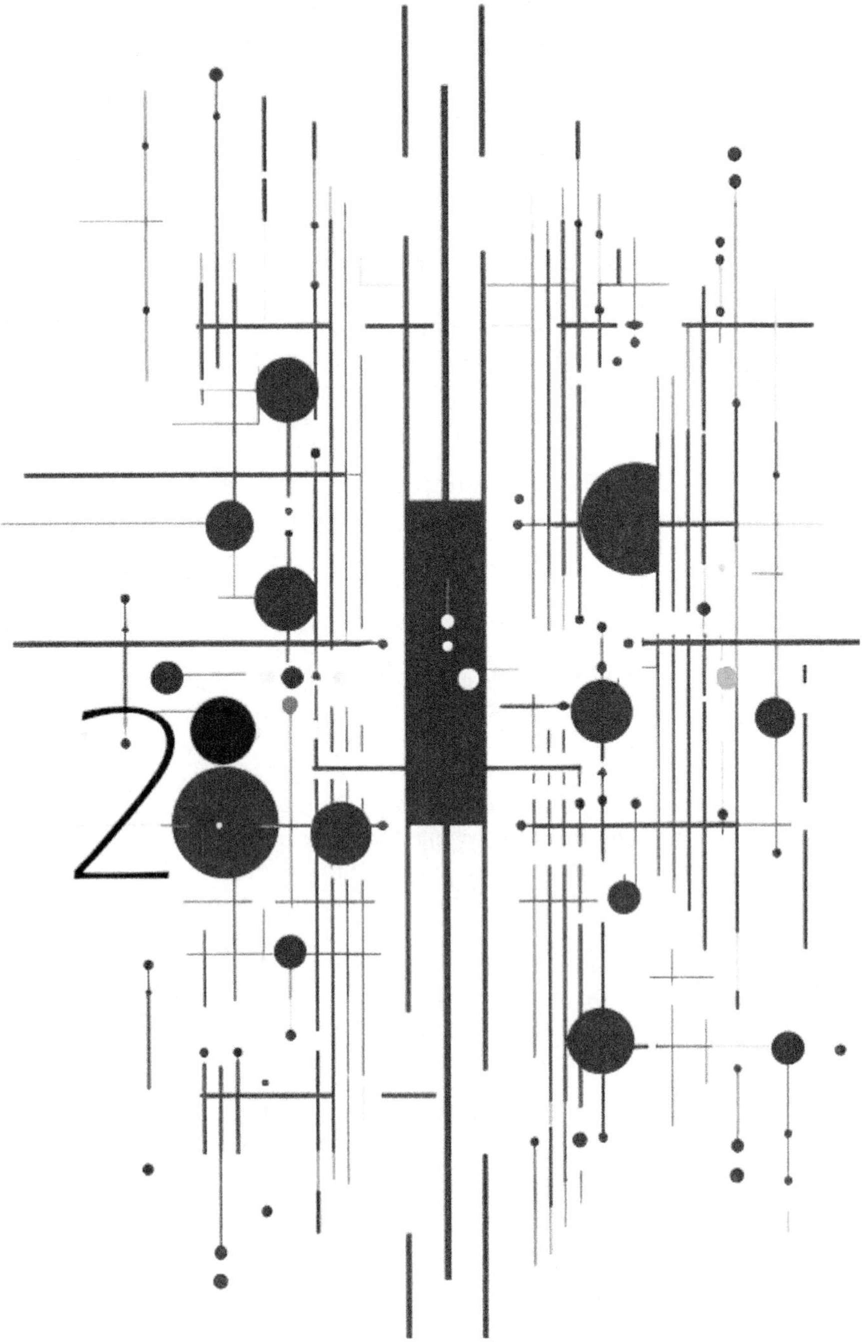
2

40
MANIFESTING WITH 28

In frequencies, where dreams take root and thoughts take flight,
a sacred pattern of life is weaved with sheer delight.
Manifesting abundance, a sacred dance we weave,
where intentions converge, and aspirations conceive.

Twenty-eight, a number whispered by fate's call,
a symbol of abundance, standing tall.
In cycles of growth and blessings untold,
a doorway to prosperity and blessing unfold.

Amid the cosmic web, a blueprint gleams,
a sacred design, woven in our dreams.
Abundance's tapestry, intricate and rare,
is a gift from the universe, beyond compare.

Now, close your eyes and breathe the air so pure,
connect with that blueprint, serene and sure.
A mantra for money, like a river's gentle flow,
"I welcome abundance, I watch it steadily grow."

With each step you take, with purpose and grace,
visualize your desires in the Universes embrace.
In your heart, let the mantra echo strong,
a harmonious melody, a prosperous throng.

Open your arms, let the energy align,
as galaxies of stars above you shine.
The sacred blueprint's power, a force untamed,
manifesting abundance, as if it were already claimed.

Embrace the number 28, a beacon so bright,
let it guide your path with its gentle light.
In this dance of creation, you hold the key,
to unlock the doors of abundance, wild and free.

So, weave your intentions with threads of light,
dance to the rhythm of abundance, day and night.
With mantra in heart, and spirit as guide,
manifesting riches is like the ocean's endless tide.

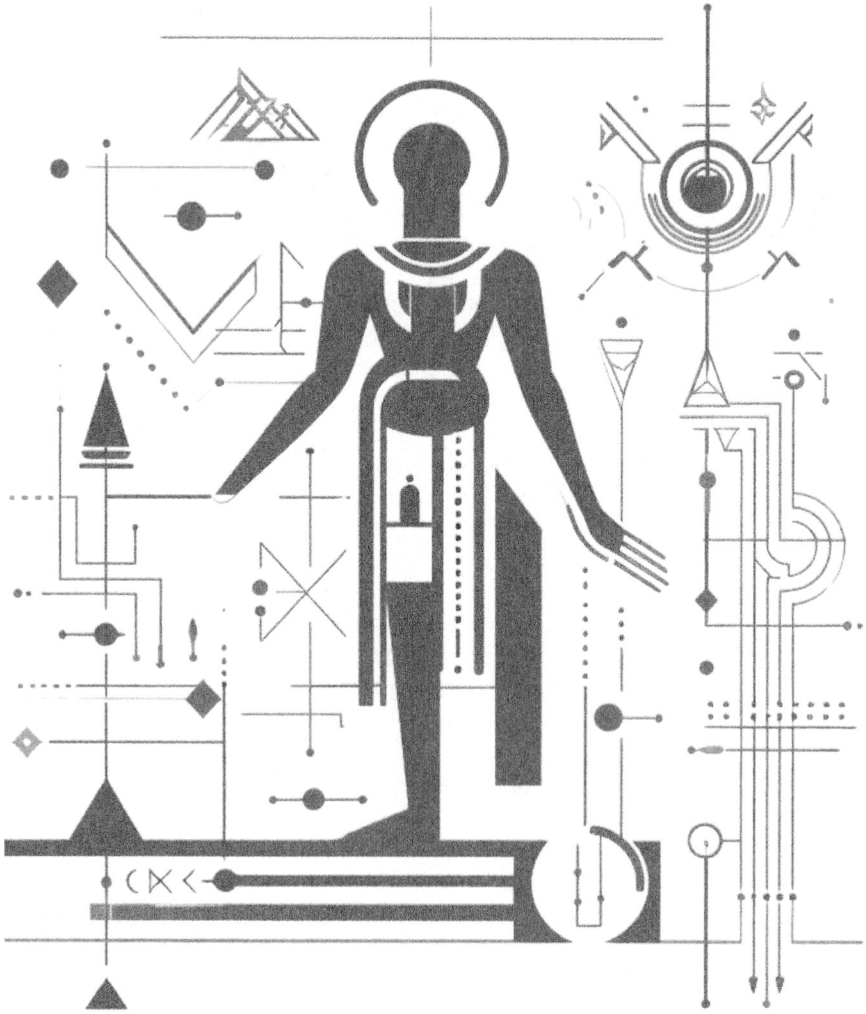

41
EMERALD TABLET

In ages past, a tablet green did rise,
with Thoth's teachings, his secrets in disguise.
The Emerald Tablet, a treasure of old,
its wisdom is woven in words of gold.

True it is, without falsehood, certain and most true,
Thoth's words begin, with clarity anew.
As above, so below, the cosmic dance,
a principle of life's intricate expanse.

Within the Tablet's verses, we are told,
of transmutation's art, as pure as gold.
Changing base to noble, lead to bright,
alchemy's secret is a mystical flight.

"Separate the subtle from the gross,"
Thoth's command was an alchemical dose.
Through distillation in fire's embrace,
purification's path becomes a sacred space.

"Understand, thou art born of the Earth and the Sky,"
a reminder profound, as time passes us by.
Human and divine, a union so true,
in our essence we find cosmic wisdom's hue.

"Sun is its father, moon its mother,"
celestial forces, one like none other.
Their harmony shapes all that we see,
in nature's tapestry, a wonderful symphony.

"Master the cycles, embrace the change,"
Thoth advises, a lesson so strange.
From death to life, and life to death,
life's eternal cycle continues with every breath.

"Focus your thoughts, with intention's might,"
mental alchemy becomes a wondrous sight.
Thoughts shape reality, a truth so pure,
manifesting dreams, like magic's lure.

So heed these teachings from the Emerald Tablet's grace,
Thoth's wisdom transcending all time and space.
As above, so below, the mysteries unfold,
in Thoth's sacred words there is treasure to behold.

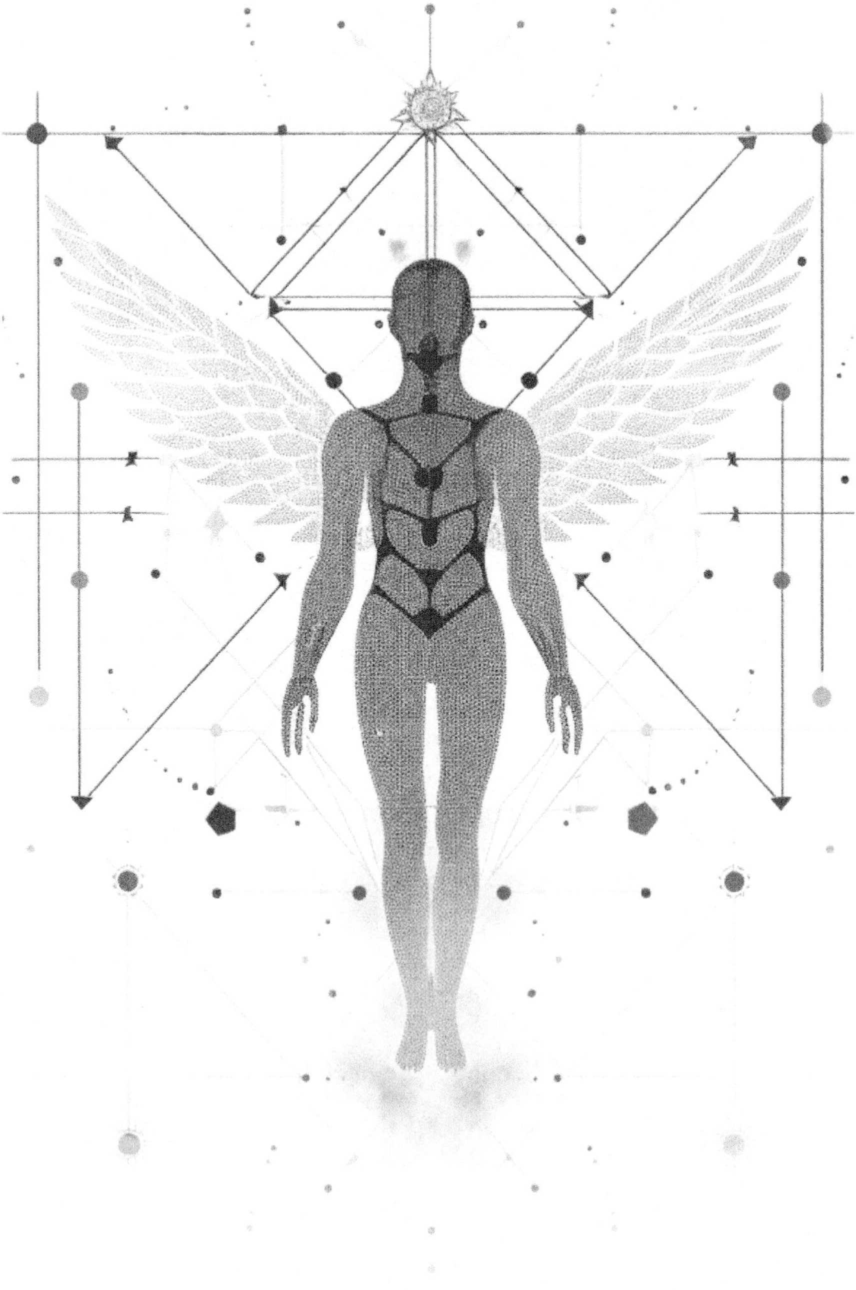

42
METATRON'S CUBE

Metatron, angel of the cube so sacred,
guide us through the portal unaffected.
To access the records of the ages,
of all that was and still engages.

The cube of light, a symbol so divine,
it holds the knowledge of all space and time.
Encoded in its facets and lines,
lies the the truth that forever shines.

To connect with it, we must raise our vibration,
purify our thoughts, and quiet our sensation.
Meditate upon the cube with intention,
then invite Metatron to our attention.

He will show us the way to the records,
through the cube, a gateway to the chord.
Of the Universe's infinite wisdom,
and the secrets of our souls' kingdom.

So let us connect with this sacred cube,
and allow Metatron to help us imbue.
With the knowledge of the akashic records,
and the understanding that life affords.

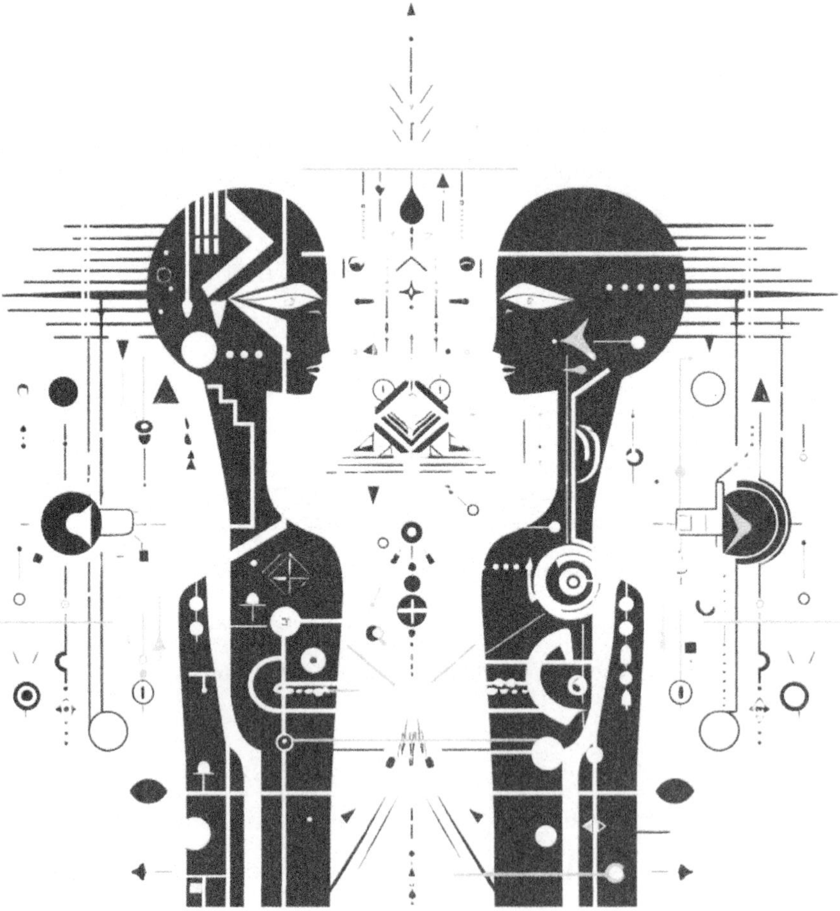

43
PLEIADEANS

In the distant cosmos, beyond our sight,
there exists a star cluster shining bright.
The Pleiadeans dwell within this celestial zone,
a race of beings with knowledge to be shown.

Their presence is felt by those who seek,
a higher consciousness, a mystical peek.
The Pleiadeans hold ancient keys,
to activate our ka, if we please.

The ka is a template within our soul,
a blueprint of life, our unseen goal.
When activated, it unleashes power,
and transforms us into a higher flower.

The Pleiadeans, with their cosmic might,
can help us find this ka light.
With their guidance, we can unlock,
our potential, like our cosmic flock.

So seek the Pleiadeans in your mind,
and let their wisdom unbind.
Unleash the ka within, and set it free,
to a higher state of being, we can be.

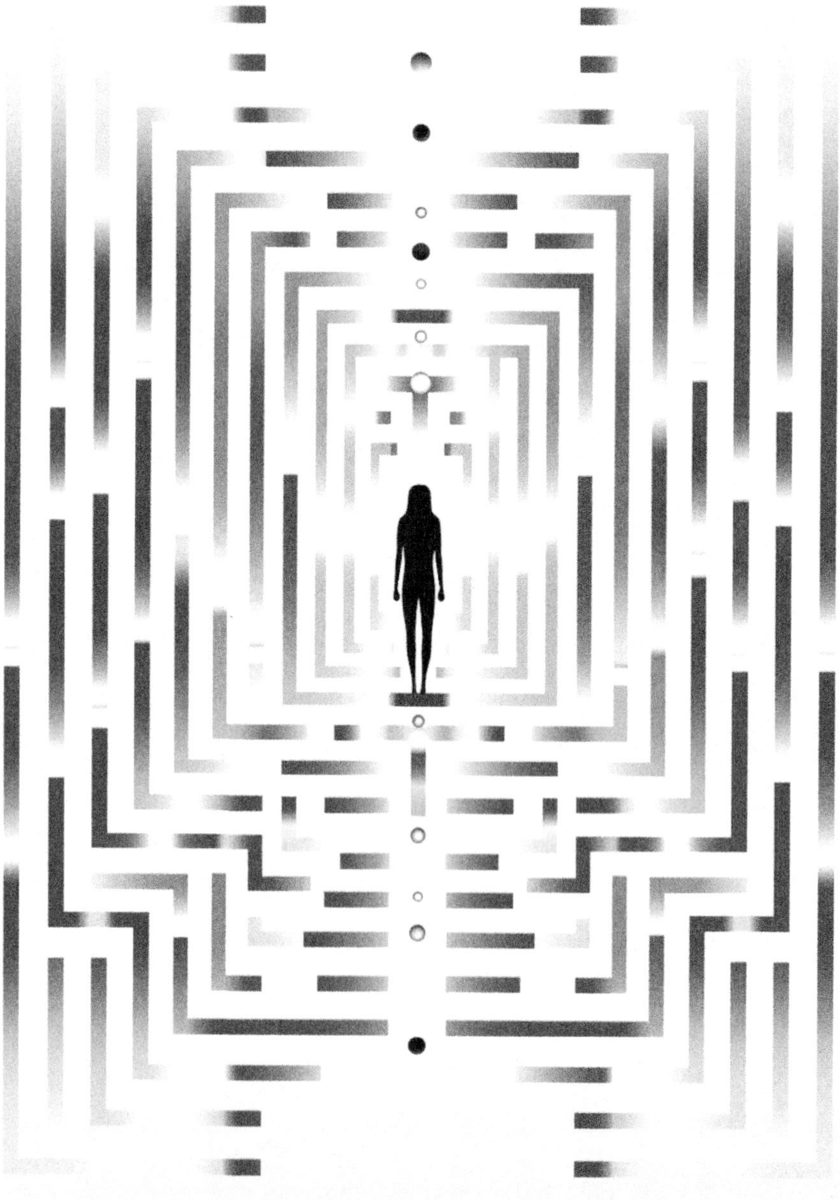

44
HEALING IN LABRYNTHS

In the heart of the labyrinth,
amidst the twists and turns.
Lies the secrets of the ages,
of the wisdom that one learns.

The path may seem confusing,
as it winds its way around.
But with each step, the answers come,
and new insights are found.

For the labyrinth holds the key,
to unlocking hidden doors.
To understanding the mysteries,
that lie deep within our cores.

In its winding, serpentine path,
we confront our deepest fears.
As we find the courage to face them,
we shed our doubts and tears.

It teaches us to trust ourselves,
and to listen to our hearts.
To release the burdens of the past,
and make a brand new start.

For in the center of the maze,
is exactly where the healing lies.
Its where we find the peace we seek,
and the light that never dies.

So walk the labyrinth with grace,
with an open mind and heart.
Now let its secrets guide you,
as you make a brand new start.

NOTES

NOTES

NOTES

NOTES

NOTES

NOTES

Printed in Great Britain
by Amazon